To Mom, Dad and Dayna

for Logan & the Hunters

Acknowledgments

No book is possible without the efforts and collaboration of many people, especially a book such as this one which developed over a period of five years. I wish first to thank Don Dansereau who as a friend and co-researcher helped design and elaborate many of the techniques presented in the book. Another friend, Sam Lane, also helped by using a typed version of the book in his classes, providing valuable insights and devoting much time and energy to make the publication a reality. Thanks also go to Lance Buhl, Delayne Hudspeth, Thaddeus O'Brien and David Watterson, all of whom read the manuscript and gave valuable feedback as well as encouragement and unwavering support. I am grateful to Deborah Freed and Mary Poole who typed earlier versions of the book. Special thanks are due Latryl Ohendalski, my editor, for her patience in guiding a new author through the details and pitfalls of publication, and also to Judy Oelfke Smith for her fine design work.

There are three major contributors to whom I am indebted. Rev Mullins, of Kansas City, my co-author, is a professional writer who reworked the book from A to Z, abbreviating my longwinded academic style, giving Nurf a genuine personality and inventing Gorbish — and best of all, adding considerable humor and sparkle. Talented artist Johnny Pate prepared the cartoons. His visualizations of the book's characters, his wit and inventiveness, added impact and life.

My final collaborator didn't rework the book or draw cartoons, but she did have the patience to put up with me for five years while all of the writing and editing was occurring. And very quietly, without fanfare, she read all versions of the manuscripts, helped type parts of them, gave her own insights, suggestions and support — and gave of her own time to free my time to write. Thanks Dayna!

Contents

Introduction

Well, how do you like it so far? (Attention getting gambit No. 1: Ask a question.) If your answer was "It seems a little brief," you can be sure of one thing: You have read and correctly digested the first eight words.

Okay, now that your interest is firmly hooked, I'm going to tell you what this book is about, how I believe it can help you stop studying and start learning and some of the things you can do to make learning easier and more fun.

I ask only one thing (Attention getting gambit No. 2: Arouse curiosity). I ask that you recognize the suggestions and techniques I offer do work and that you can use them now and become a better learner.

Well, I suppose those were two things. That was pretty sneaky of me. But in return for reading this far, I'll make you a promise: When you finish reading this book, you won't just know how to improve your learning, you will have become a better learner.

Now to get you to finish the book, I must get and keep your attention. I plan to do that with all sorts of underhanded little devices, like Nurf and Gorbish (characters whom you will meet later), a whole passel of Fenker's Facilitating Facts, typeface changes, a few cockleburrs placed under the saddle, a booby trap here and there, pitfalls, deadfalls, short-circuits and the like. You know, just good-old-honest-American fun. And the reason I am doing

this is that I want to keep your mind going in high gear.

I believe this book will succeed because it's a book that will keep you doing instead of just reading. And if it can do that, you will be a better learner.

Now, you have a choice; read and become a better learner or quit somewhere

Dr. Fenker

1

down the line. If you choose the latter, you will, I predict, have a miserable life and be afflicted with warts, wens and boils, not to mention a visitation of locust and acute athlete's foot. So don't take a chance.

Now you ask (go ahead, I don't mind questions), "Who is this Fenker, and what are his credentials for writing a book on learning?"

I'm glad you asked that: I am a psychologist and a teacher. All of those long tedious years while my friends were reading *Penthouse*, hanging toy monkeys on the rear vision mirrors of their Alpha Romeos and making fortunes practicing the basic tenets of the free enterprise system, I was doing something else — doggedly studying, spending countless hours in libraries, implementing test programs on unsuspecting students and figuring percentages on the back of my shovel with a piece of charcoal. And hating every minute of it.

When I finally received a Ph.D. and began my teaching career, I discovered an amazing fact: I wasn't the only person who didn't like studying! In fact, almost none of my students enjoyed it. On the other hand, most of them (and I) enjoyed learning. But when learning involved anything as distasteful as studying, I did my best to avoid it or to make it as painless as possible.

What emerged was a collection of techniques that permitted me either to avoid completely tasks that feel like studying or to deal with them quickly and painlessly.

Big deal, Fenker. Your credentials are

about as impressive as those of Elizabeth Taylor's marriage counselor.

Nurf

Oh, hello, Nurf. I figured you'd show up sooner or later. Friends, this is Nurf. Every teacher (sigh) has a Nurf in one of his classes. You'll note that he speaks in bold Italican and has a remarkable talent for untimely interruptions and questions, and in general, has a nasty turn of mind.

Save your pretty words, Fenker. I'm here to keep you honest, if that word is in your vocabulary. And Ph.D.? That doesn't spell anything.

Wait, Nurf, you've missed the point. My credentials are simply that I dislike activities that feel like studying. And because of that, I have developed an incredible collection of techniques for avoiding studying and improving learning. During the past ten years I've been teaching these techniques to high school and college students, as well as to adults. And, to my delight and their[1] surprise, the methods work!

Gorbish

This is attention getting gambit No. 3: The Footnote. The voice from the pit is that of Gorbish, our computer, who also exhibits some of Nurf's less desirable characteristics. He is, I must admit, saturated in his circuitry with information about learning. Some is important. Some is as useless as a training bra for Dolly Parton.

GORBISH is the acronym for:
GASEOUS DISPLAY
OPTICAL READING
RANDOM ACCESS
BINARY
INTEGRATING
SELECTIVE
HISTORYBANK

Gorbish is fully automatic, beyond my control and is on hair-trigger alert to respond to omitted details and statements which may be wanting in total accuracy. He is also arrogant, pretentious and pompous, thus making one long for the days when computers ran on coal oil. Now, where was I?

You don't remember where you are, and you want people to trust your book on learning?

Oh, Yes. You might have thought you

---

[1]"Their" refers to the students and adults who used Dr. Fenker's techniques and were amazed at the results. You will note that Dr. Fenker is often quite vague in his pronoun references. This is a trait exhibited in many post-doctoral periods by those who have become expert in a specific field but who have never mastered the simple eighth-grade art of diagramming an easy sentence. One wonders.

bought a book on learning. This is partially true, but it's also about traveling, imagination, sports, problem solving, relaxation and a number of other interesting subjects.

The book, you will notice, has four major themes. First, in a number of places it compares learning with taking a trip. The process of learning is compared to traveling, while achieving a learning goal is compared to reaching your destination. Building on this analogy, most learners in America's school systems have spent the majority of their lives traveling without ever looking out the window!

High schools and colleges teach us to think of learning as attaining certain goals — passing tests, writing papers, finishing assignments, completing classes, getting a diploma or a job. And they pay virtually no attention to how we get to these goals, that is, the nature of the learning process.

So, just as the length and pleasantness of a trip depend both on the driver's skill and the route selected, your effectiveness as a learner and the enjoyment you get from learning depend on your skill at mastering the process of learning.

In other words, this book encourages you to become aware of how you are learning, instead of only what you are learning. I want you to look at the scenery outside your window on your learning trip. It's not a waste of time. Far from it. Understanding and using effective learning methods to your own advantage is one of the keys to enjoying your life both in school and afterward.

The second theme is that learners are very different individuals. Each has his or her own unique intellectual makeup, experiences, learning style and goals or directions. Because of this, no two individuals will ever start or finish a learning trip at exactly the same place.

I tried to write a book that was flexible enough to fit the diversity of styles, interests, backgrounds, and yes, even degrees of laziness of the readers.[1] Thus, out of the large collection of ideas, suggestions or techniques that I offer, you may find only a few that seem appropriate or workable for you. Trust your intuition. If the technique doesn't feel right or meet your needs, then don't try and force it. On the other hand, keep an open mind, and don't let laziness prevent you from using a method that you know can help. Also, as you become a better learner, your attitudes about the usefulness of some techniques will change.

Third, learning is easier and more fun if you use both sides of your brain. The left side which is responsible for speech and reasoning ability, is where most of your education has been focused. But I believe it is essential to combine those skills with the right-brain's powers of imagination, intuition, visualization and holistic perception.

Last, the most effective learners are indi-

---

[1] Dr. Fenker's laziness quotient, as measured on the Freen-Trafney Sloth Scale, falls off the chart. This data has been confirmed in countless observations by Dr. Fenker's wife, Dayna, who is regularly forced to take his pulse to determine if he is among the quick or the dead.

viduals operating primarily under their own control. This is in contrast to the controls or directions imposed by parents, teachers, employers, friends or the environment.

Clearly, as a student and citizen, you must deal with homework assignments, job requirements, traffic tickets and the IRS (to mention only a few). But, the point is, if you face each situation and make your own decisions about what you want, rather than passively accepting what comes, you're much more likely to be happy and successful. When you decide what you want to achieve, then the job of traveling or completing a task will be more enjoyable. And your final destination will be much closer to your original goals.

Thus, my objective is not to make you an "A" student. Rather, I want you to decide if the effort required to make an "A" is worthwhile. Then, if your answer is "Yes," I'll provide you with the travel skills necessary to reach this destination. If the answer is "No," then I'll show you some other methods for speeding up the trip so you can reach the quickest acceptable destination — perhaps a "B" or a "C" or even a "D".

While much of this book is oriented to high school and college learning problems, it also applies to sports learning and to any form of job or skill training.

Now, let's fire up the engine. But remember, we're in no hurry to finish. The travel aids and maps provided represent a fine set of tools, but they do require some time to practice and master. So relax, roll down the windows of your car on both sides, drop into high gear, and let's enjoy the trip.

Chapter 1

Two Brains Are Better Than One

(Especially if they're packed in the same skull)

Suppose I told you that:

1. You actually have two different minds, not just one.
2. Your formal education in grade school, high school, and perhaps college, has been focused on developing only one of these minds. The other has been almost completely ignored.
3. One key to becoming a better learner is to make effective use of both minds . . . and
4. Development of the neglected mind will open the door to a world in which you can:
   a. Concentrate without being distracted.
   b. Memorize material almost effortlessly.
   c. Develop confidence in your learning abilities and eliminate tensions and anxieties connected with learning.
   d. Heighten your imagination to solve problems and think creatively.

I'd say you were probably a Grade Three Charlatan and should be tarred and sequined and ridden out of town in a '55 Nash station wagon.

Well, Nurf, you're up early in this chap-

ter. Your reaction isn't surprising. I get it from a number of people until they have finished the book. These facts do take a bit of faith to accept. But they are true. And if you are willing to help yourself, this book will show you how to achieve some of these remarkable results.

First, however, we have to build a foundation of information. You need to become familiar with such terms as self-talk, consciousness, dominant hemisphere, active and passive states of mind and sequential versus simultaneous thinking. These ideas aren't difficult, but they will require a few minutes of explanation.

Self-Talk

Let's start by tuning into Nurf's head and pick up whatever he's muttering about.

Two minds in a 7⅜ hat size! This is going to be a great book for fanning the flies off my bowl of Farina. No wonder the American educational system is up to its clavicle in problems.

Now that we have illegally bugged Nurf's head, we'll admit that such a conversation may also be taking place in your head. We all talk to ourselves. We carry on a continuous running dialogue in our heads. These conversations, which I call self-talk, serve a definite purpose. They help us sort out our feelings and thoughts about the world around us.

Okay, so I talk to myself. But who's listening? I am, and that's a total of one, not two people.

Count again, Nurf. There's a good chance that the TALKER and the LISTENER inside your head represent different entities. They certainly don't always agree. And, as you will see below, they have quite different personalities. Can't you remember a time when the TALKER did its best to persuade the LISTENER about a particular decision, but the LISTENER would not agree? And, as a result, the decision never "felt" quite right.

Let's try our first experiment. The object: to turn off the TALKER. Find a quiet, comfortable place where you will not be disturbed. Sit or lie down and let your body relax. Now, allow the constant self-talk in your mind to gradually quieten until it finally disappears. Let your mind become blank, like a clean slate. Try this for two minutes. (I'll wait.)

Time's up. You found it didn't work? Not surprising. Most people find this simple exercise impossible without considerable practice and training in meditative techniques. Except in the sleep state, it's a difficult task to quiet the TALKER.

Now, let's try again, but this time, concentrate on repeating silently to yourself a special word. Let's use a soft, pleasant word like "murmur." Repeat it silently, over and over. Did you do a little better? Focusing makes it easier to exclude everything else and arrive at a blank mind.

Who's talking, who's listening?

Your brain is divided into two hemispheres, right and left. They are connected by a bundle of nerve fibers called the corpus collosum. It operates like a telephone cable sending thousands of words a minute back and forth, keeping the two hemispheres in constant communication. Scientists believe that the left side of the brain houses the higher cortical functions.

Attaboy, Fenker. Let's impress everyone with your education.

Sorry, Nurf. It just slipped out. Higher cortical functions simply means speech, verbal skills, logical reasoning, and analytical thinking. Each of these functions is believed to be associated with the left hemisphere or the TALKER. The TALKER dominates our perception of the world with its constant verbal activity. The right hemisphere, while less well understood, is thought to be responsible for spatial reasoning, visualization, and creativity. It's also the LISTENER, the part of the brain that "hears" the TALKER's constant dialog.

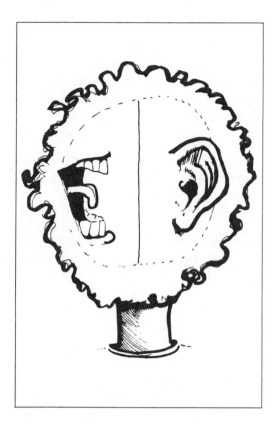

Just how much of this are you making up, Fenker?[1]

Thank you, Gorbish. Now, to continue. Since both sides are normally active to some extent, we usually describe the hemisphere which is controlling your conscious activity at any moment as the dominant hemisphere. And further, associated with a particular hemisphere being dominant is a unique state of mind or consciousness.

There are many such states. Your normal, everyday, waking consciousness is probably the most familiar. In this state, life is a continual series of activities: eating, reading, walking, talking, watching TV, etc. Your consciousness or your attention is directed toward these activities. Also, the *TALKER* is usually busy controlling, guiding or evaluating what's happening.

Another state of mind is more passive. It's associated with "sensing" your surroundings — attending to the sounds, tastes, smells, touch — without much verbal thought. This is typically a relaxed state in which you become primarily a receiver of information about the world rather than an actor or manipulator.

The active state of mind, your normal consciousness, occurs when the left hemisphere is dominant. Conversely, the right hemisphere is dominant during the more passive, receptive states of consciousness.

Okay, Fenker, left-brain: TALKER, active, dominant. Right-brain: LISTENER, passive, receptive. Can't you ever get to the point?

---

[1] Let me respond to Mr. Nurf's pecksniffery. I find mental grappling with him like unto toying with an infant. Dr. Fenker is entirely correct; and I cite, as his authority, studies by Sperry, Milner and Strong. I trust, Dr. Fenker, you will not mind if I interrupt from time to time, drawing from the infinite wellspring of my infallible information which I have at the tip of my transistors, to squelch the inane comments of this barbarian. I feel . . .

Coming up, Nurf. I'm going to show you why this passive state is important to learning. The first step is to demonstrate the important connection between your "two brains", and this involves understanding the language of each.

Sequential vs. Simultaneous

The language of the left-brain is no problem. It's the common, ordinary speech we use every day with words, sentences and grammatical rules to provide structure. You know this language well, because, as I mentioned earlier, 95 per cent of your formal education has made use of it for reading, writing, speaking and reasoning.

Left-brain thinking is logical, orderly and sequential. We create sentences word by word and paragraphs, sentence by sentence. We combine the units of language bit by bit until they form a complete thought or idea.

And here's where the trouble comes when you're trying to learn complex new material or trying to make a difficult, personal decision. There is so much information you can lose track of the sequence. You try to fit ideas and data together in a logical manner, and what happens? Because of their complexity, your thoughts become a jumble, instead of flowing smoothly to a conclusion.

Now, let me dangle something entrancingly enticing before you, Nurf. Wouldn't it be great if we had a language that was simultaneous, instead of sequential? If,

instead of receiving information piece by piece or word by word, it all came at once — zap, bang, instantaneously?

Well, that's where the right-brain comes in, for its language is thought to be just that, simultaneous in nature.

Fenker, I'm listening, but I don't hear a simultaneous language. You're talking word by word like everyone else.

That's because you don't know what to listen for. The only language you're used to hearing is the left-brain's language which consists of words and sentences. These thoughts spread over time like footsteps across space. Each must start at some point and finish at another point some time or some distance later.

Unfortunately, the *TALKER*, using its left-brain language, makes a great deal of noise. And so if we want to hear or make use of the right-brain's powerful instantaneous language, we've got to somehow shut off the *TALKER*.

This is the importance of right-brained states of consciousness, ones in which the *TALKER* is silenced. By turning off the *TALKER*, we get all of the information at once without our minds being encumbered with the thousands of words needed to describe a situation or problem.

Come out from under that disguise, Fenker. I see the old snake oil peddler. Good for man and beast, cures everything from hives to hernias. I'll know to keep

10

*my hand on my wallet and my Zig-Zags
whenever I'm around you.* [1]

No fairy tales, Nurf. What I am saying
is that the right-brain's language is one of
images instead of words. Images, by definition, give you a view of the whole picture instead of a log jam of pieces. What's
an image? It's usually some form of mental picture or visualization. But images can
also represent feelings or abstract ideas.

Suppose I asked you to imagine the
faces on Mt. Rushmore. Some of you will
be able to instantly create a clear, vivid,
dreamlike picture in your minds. Others
will be able to muster only the fuzziest of
scenes.

*Reading from left to right, I get Wash-
ington, Jefferson, Lincoln and Elton John.*

Not bad, Nurf. Most people list Washington, Jefferson, Lincoln and Groucho
Marx. But the point is this: Imagery is a
learned skill. You'll get better with practice. On the other hand, if you are unable
to form clear mental pictures, don't worry.
This doesn't imply that you are unskilled
at using the right-brain's image language.

That's an elephant?

Remember the old parable about the
three blind men encountering an elephant
for the first time. One, grabbing its tail,
concluded the elephant was like a rope.
The second touched its trunk and decided
it was like a snake. The third, running
into a leg, pictured the elephant as a tree
trunk.

That is left-brain or piece-by-piece perception. A sighted person would have
seen the elephant in its six-ton entirety at
one glance. And that's right-brain perception or simultaneous sensing.

But, let's not get hung up on pictures.
Many of these images that comprise the
right-brain's language are not mental pictures, but are more like patterns of
thoughts or collections of feelings, ideas
and experiences. The point to remember is
that the left-brain's language puts together
parts to make a whole. In right-brain language, the whole is there to begin with. [2]

Now, it's time for another experiment.
Quiet your mind. Let it focus on the "total" image of a parent or close friend. Say
that person's name to yourself. Let your
mind embrace the total range of feelings,
experiences, fantansies and visual impressions associated with this person.

---

[1]Calumny! My accurate records show Dr. Fenker has no history of theft, petty or grand larceny,
although some law enforcement agencies list in his description the phrase "shifty-eyed."

[2]May I elaborate, Dr. Fenker? This is called "wholistic" thinking (sometimes spelled "holistic"). A
very impressive term used to describe these wholistic images is "Gestalt." I mention this so Dr.
Fenker can feel secure that whenever he fails to include some important thought or data, I will be
here to bail him out or straighten out the confusion he has created.

Now, notice that these separate images, experiences and ideas do not in any sense need to be combined to form the person's total image in your mind. The image is "whole" to begin with. You can deal with the parts by forcing your attention in specific directions. When was the last time you wrote home? Remember how his voice sounded in your ear while you were dancing? Observe that the parts flow from the entire image, rather than being added, to create it.

Next, let's try the other side of the coin. Imagine how you would describe this parent or friend to a third person. Imagine the endless collection of descriptive statements — looks, job, address, attitudes, abilities — you would need to construct even a very sketchy picture in the third person's mind. This additive, sequential, building process characterizes left-brain thinking. See how slow and incomplete it seems compared to the images of right-brain thinking.

Fenker, you've made your point. Only last night I was trying to give a young lady, my lovely Aureola, a view of my attributes — the brilliance of my mind, the acuity of my intelligence, the tanned and muscled perfection of my lithe body, the myriad of talents I am bringing to the peak of perfection. It was a staggering task and took so long that what I be-lieved to be an anticipatory growl in her throat proved to be only snoring. Tonight I will zap her with the old right-brain concept.[1]

Of course, we all utilize both right and left-brain thought processes in our everyday lives. Certain kinds of educational experiences in art, math, athletics and other subjects do directly or indirectly develop right-brain thought processes. But, because the majority of our formal education is focused solely on left-brain skills, it is likely your right-brain abilities are undeveloped. And, before you finish this book, you're going to give those abilities a real workout.

Now, let's sequentially and left-brainedly confirm our major points (because that's the way you are currently best at learning):

1. Your left-brain is the *TALKER*, primarily responsible for speech, verbal skills, logical reasoning and sequential thinking.
2. Your right-brain is the *LISTENER* and represents a more passive, receptive state of mind, associated with intuition, feeling, hunches and imagination. It perceives the world in non-verbal images which are often (but not always) visual in nature.
3. Right-brain processes have a whole, in-

---

[1]Microcomputation of the time to sequentially enumerate Mr. Nurf's meritorious attributes in detail comes to a minuscule 4.183 seconds, with time left over for a stifled yawn.

tegrated character as contrasted with the part-by-part sequential thinking of the left-brain.

4. Right-brain states can be achieved through relaxation or meditation. More of this is coming up in the next chapter.

Now, fasten your seat belt because we're going to learn how to get maximum mileage out of these learning processes that have been lying in disuse for so long.

Chapter 2

Right Brain, Right On!

How to Get There Without Even Trying

Time to go back into the Famous Fenker Laboratory. We open the squeaking door, light the candle, brush aside the cobwebs and wait for the rushing wings of the bats to still.

From the dust-covered instrument cabinet, we take two objects — a golden ring and a string some eight inches long. Now, I want you to tie the string to the ring and hold the free end of the string between your thumb and forefingers.

Steady now. You will notice it is impossible to keep the pendulum from moving just a little. Now, imagine the pendulum moving from side to side. Watch it closely. See what's happening? It is now doing just that.

Now, imagine the pendulum moving in a circle. Concentrate. The pattern is changing. The pendulum is now going around and around.

Now, visualize the pendulum swinging to and from you, back and forth in a straight line. Concentrate on this movement. The pattern now is changing just as you pictured.

What's happening in this simple exercise?

You're auditioning for the third remake of "Frankenstein meets Donnie Osmond."

No, Nurf, my agent closed that deal last week. You can check "Variety." There is a simple answer. Remember, in Chapter 1 you learned the left-brain uses a language of words and the right-brain uses a language of images? If you simply said to yourself "I am going to make the pendulum move from side to side," then the left-brain was in control. If, on the other hand, you formed an image of the pendulum moving from side to side, then the right-brain used this image to instruct your muscles how to move.

Come on, Fenker. Are you telling me that my subconscious mind moved the pendulum?

Well, you're clearly conscious of wanting the pendulum to move. But you're not telling yourself with words to move it. Instead, you're using a mental picture. I don't think this makes it a subconscious process, but rather a different kind of conscious activity than we are used to monitoring. It's a type of consciousness where the *TALKER* is less in control.

Well, if I can do that, I think I'll sell my car jack.

Hold off, Nurf. I'm not claiming you can move mountains with the mind. But the images formed by your right-brain can do a lot more than move a pendulum. In fact, once you learn to control such images they can help you concentrate, think creatively, solve problems, take exams without anxiety and do all of the other things I promised you a while ago.

I'll keep the tire jack. But, turn over the shells in your little game and show me where the pea is.

Okay, let's take a look. The major problem in using your right-brain is learning how to communicate with it. And there's a technique for doing this. The technique involves "tuning" out the state associated with the dominant left hemisphere. This is a passive process which depends more on "letting go" of your everyday waking consciousness than it does on "doing something" with your right-brain. Put simply, it means you must allow the *TALKER* to be silent.

The process of "tuning out" the *TALKER* might be compared to stepping out of the bright sunlight into the semi-darkness of a movie theater.[1] As long as the *TALKER* is in control, you can't see clearly enough to make use of the full powers of your right-brain. You may be aware of the "shapes" such as intuition, imagery, or creativity lurking in the background. But, it's difficult to shut out the sunlight in order to perceive these shapes clearly.

This question of control can be the most important problem you face as a learner. What does control mean to you?

Easy, Man. I'm in control when I've got my roommate bound and gagged, the TV off, a jug of Ripple in one hand and Aureola in the other.

This isn't the chapter on fantasies. But most of my students would probably agree with you. To them, "control" means

---

[1]For the readers' edification, I happen to know this analogy was lifted . . . and grotesquely distorted . . . from Robert Ornstein's excellent book, *Psychology of Consciousness*. You readers needn't worry, I'll keep an eye on Dr. Fenker all the way through this thing.

dealing with something external to themselves such as finding a place to study, turning off the TV, hushing a noisy roommate, having the right book or notes to review for an exam, impressing your teachers or using good study techniques. Most books on "How to Learn" focus primarily on just such external kinds of control.

And you're putting down these other books?

Not at all. Some of them work very well. But because they concern things external to you, they represent control only in the left-brain sense; that is, they are a part of the TALKER's constant attempts to act on or manipulate the world around you.

There is another type of control which is vital for effective learning — internal control. This means control of the world inside your head. Normally, this is a more passive type of control which involves sensing, feeling, monitoring and altering — often through images — your internal world. And this type of control is associated with the right-brain.

How does internal control affect learning? Well, there are many ways, and I've listed them at the end of this chapter. But a few of the most important include:[1]

- the ability to concentrate
- the ability to relax and deal effectively with tensions, anxieties and high pressure situations
- the ability to develop and use visual imagery skills
- the ability to eliminate self-doubts and negative thoughts.

To attain these internal controls, you need to tune out the left-brain and tune in the right.

Three roads to the right

How do we get there! Well, there are many methods, but the most common are self-hypnotic procedures and meditative techniques. These are the vehicles that will carry you into the "twilight" of right-brain consciousness.

I'm about to enter still another state of consciousness, Fenker — sleep. Get on with it before I nod off completely.

Don't go to sleep on me, Nurf. Relax! Just relax, because now we're going to get

---

[1]In his haste, Dr. Fenker omitted many metaphysical schools, religious organizations, psychological growth-oriented groups, hypnotic societies and "mind-control" businesses which offer techniques for using the intuitive, subconscious mind. These groups or philosophies include Yoga, Hinduism, Builders of the Adytum, Silva Mind Control, Scientology, Transcendental Meditation, Zen, Sufism and Krishna. I told you I'd keep an eye on him!

into it — a basic progressive relaxation technique. It's going to open a whole new world for you. So relax; and yet, be alert while I outline it. It's an easy way to reach a right-brain state of consciousness if you will practice it for a couple of weeks. And, it will be one of the best investments you could ever make in becoming a more effective learner. I recommend it because:

- It's simple and straightforward
- It doesn't require a commitment to a particular religious or metaphysical school of thought
- It can be easily learned and experienced by most people in a relatively short time (one or two weeks) and
- It can be learned, with practice, on your own without the assistance of a teacher.

OMMM....

Okay, here it is:

1. Find a place where you can sit comfortably and not be disturbed for 15 to 20 minutes. If possible, this place should be away from the television, the telephone, voices of friends and other things which are likely to disturb you or require your attention. After some practice, you may find it possible to relax in a noisy atmosphere; but while learning, it is best to be as quiet and undisturbed as possible.

2. You may choose to lie prone or sit. If prone, lie flat on your back with arms at your side. If sitting, find a chair with a back that can support your head and neck.

3. To increase your awareness of the difference between relaxed and tense muscular states, do the following:
Tighten the muscles in your feet for a few seconds. Now, release this tension. Let the muscles relax. Notice what it feels like for your legs to be relaxed. Now, repeat this exercise with your arms and hands. Repeat it once more with your shoulders, neck and head. In each case, let the tension and tightness flow away when you relax the muscles.
Let your eyelids close gently. Notice as your eyelids relax, they become heavier and very limp. You don't make any conscious effort to keep your eyes closed. As your eyelids relax, your eyes will close of their own accord.

4. Now, inhale deeply and exhale slowly and smoothly. As you exhale, mentally say to yourself the word, "relax." Feel all the tension and tightness in your body flowing outward as you exhale. Repeat this exercise for several breaths until your entire body feels relaxed and free from tension.

5. Next, mentally scan each part of your body, willing it to relax completely. Start with your toes and work slowly upward. Focus on your:
— toes
— feet
— ankles
— calves
— knees
— upper legs
— thighs
— hips
— abdomen
— stomach
— chest
— back
— shoulders
— arms
— hands
— neck
— jaw
— cheeks
— forehead
— scalp

6. Say to yourself, "My whole body is now deeply and healthily relaxed. If I notice any tension, I can simply focus on that part of my body, and the tension will disappear. If any sounds or distractions enter my consciousness, I will make no effort to respond to them or worry about them. Instead, I will simply allow them to drift away, much as a cloud drifts through the sky on a sunny day."

7. Now relax yourself even more deeply by slowly counting from 10 down to 1. With each number, feel yourself sinking deeper and deeper into a healthy, relaxed state. Feel your body become very limp and almost numb as your consciousness pulls away from your muscles and senses and focuses inward.

8. When you reach the count of 1, you are completely relaxed and in a right-brain state of consciousness. This is the time to work out any problems that may be bothering you, to mentally rehearse a sport, to reduce tensions and anxieties about a coming exam, to practice your imagery skills, or simply to rest. The comments you make to yourself during this period should be positive and directed toward the purpose of quieting your mind and bringing it into harmony with your feelings, desires and objectives. Examples of some comments you might use to deal with specific problems are given in the next

section of this chapter.

9. When you are ready to wake up from this very relaxed, right-brain state, I recommend the following procedure:

Take several deep breaths. Each time you inhale, imagine your lungs drawing light and energy into your body. Feel the energy spread throughout your body. As you exhale, let the stale air take with it all tiredness and tension and sickness. Breathe out tension and negative thoughts.

Now, imagine yourself rising from the depths of the ocean floor to the surface. Begin counting from 1 to 5. With each number, you become more aware of your body and the sounds around you. At 5, you break the surface of the water into a bright, beautiful day feeling refreshed but wide awake and full of energy.

Nurf? Nurf!!

Zzzzz . . .

Well, don't be surprised if this happens when you attempt to relax. It's not unusual for a relaxed state to become a sleep state for one simple reason: most people achieve deep relaxation prior to or during sleep and at no other time. With practice, the association between relaxation and sleep will weaken. And you'll find your-

self able to remain both relaxed and conscious (in a right-brain state) at the same time. Besides, you probably needed a nap anyway.

Now, don't expect to master this technique today. It will require some effort on your part — at least a couple of weeks of practice — to learn how to achieve this completely relaxed, right-brain state easily and quickly. At times, while you're learning (and even later after much experience), you may find it difficult to relax because of anxiety, a headache or a noisy environment.

Don't sweat it

If you only attain a partially relaxed state, don't worry or be upset. This state is still extremely beneficial. Your muscles and your mind are resting and being recharged.

It seems strange, but one of the major difficulties my students have while learning these methods is that anxieties about not relaxing deeply enough prevent them from relaxing more deeply. So, accept whatever level of relaxation you can attain as a useful, beneficial state. More completely relaxed states will come with practice.

Tape talk

Many people find that even when the *TALKER* is telling you to relax, the fact that it is your own voice can prevent you from reaching a deeply relaxed state. A "relaxation" tape or recording of someone[1] taking you step by step through the process of relaxing can be very helpful in these cases. There is one such tape dealing specifically with learning problems for sale in conjunction with this book. And my students who have used it have found it to be quite effective.

I knew it! Sooner or later, Fenker, I knew you would get to the old hard sell. I suppose if I listen to the tape you'll tell me to buy another copy of this book.

Just making its existence known, Nurf. In addition to my learning tape, there are many other commercially produced tapes and records for relaxation and meditation that are quite good. However, eventually you're going to want to attain this state on your own to take advantage of the unlimited possibilities it opens to you.

Okay, close the cash register; I'm ready for an incredibly refreshing study break. I deserve it for coming with you this far.

Okay, Nurf. I've got just the thing for you — a self-talk program. Self-talk programs are simply collections of statements you can tell yourself when in a relaxed, right-brained state. They can have a profound affect on how you feel. Do you want to feel refreshed, alert and able to concentrate after a study break?

Well, here's ol' Fenker's program. (You probably can construct a better one by substituting your own language and feelings. But, remember to use it after you have reached a right-brain state.)

Fenker's Relaxing, Recharging Routine

My body is completely relaxed. I feel very balanced, harmonious and quiet inside. My awareness has been withdrawn from my body and senses and is now focused inward. I feel very healthy and alert. Each day I become better and better. If I experience any pain or sickness, I can now direct the full energy of my mind toward that portion of my body needing healing. Then I will imagine the full energy of my mind joining with the body's other defenses. Even after I awake, this men-

---

[1]Guess who?

21

tal energy will continue to aid the healing process.

Before waking, I want to fill my body with energy for the next learning task. I can see that my body is surrounded by a sea of energy. As I inhale, it flows into my lungs and spreads throughout my body. As I exhale, the air takes with it all tiredness, sickness and negative feelings. Breathe in energy and freshness. Breathe out tiredness. Repeat this for a few breaths, then gently return to a normal waking state.

When you wake from a relaxed or meditative state and return to normal left-brain consciousness you'll most likely "feel better." You'll experience a sense of being refreshed, and more detached and less concerned about the world around you.

Ah, zonkedness, at last.

For you, Nurf, perhaps. But for the rest of us, a sense of well-being, of being in control of the world inside our heads. And as we'll see in the next chapters, you'll have the ability to deal with the kinds of internal hassles that interfere with learning. And that's our objective.

The possibilities for using right-brain consciousness to improve your effectiveness as a learner is nothing less than astonishing. With practice here's what you can do:

1. Quiet a noisy, distracting *TALKER* in order to concentrate (Chapter 3)
2. Help solve complicated academic and personal problems (Chapter 10)
3. Improve your performances in sports (Chapter 12)
4. Develop your ability to visualize or form mental pictures (Chapter 11)
5. Improve your memory (Chapter 6)
6. Enhance your creative abilities (Chapters 10 and 11)
7. Reduce tension and anxiety that relates to learning problems (Chapter 3)
8. Learn to take an incredibly refreshing 60-minute study break in 10 minutes (See this chapter)
9. Eliminate negative feelings about yourself, your instructors or learning activities (Chapter 3)

And win a free case of Geritol on "Bowling for Dollars."

Chapter 3

Eliminating Internal Distractors

"Shut up in there!"

"The 747 landed in the swamp in a level-descending attitude because . . . the crew was distracted.". . . synopsis of an FAA accident report.

You talk about distraction? I'll give you distraction. On a recent TV talk show, the host was interviewing one of America's top singers and asked him if he could recall his first big break on the way to stardom. What followed was a recitation of one of the most terrible moments in the man's life. After years of struggling, he was booked on one of the highest rated TV programs in Los Angeles. He was backed by a marvelous band, had great arrangements and all he had to do to establish himself as a real comer was to deliver his usual good performance.

One of his friends, with a bizarre sense of humor and no sense of responsibility, was seated on the front row of the audience. As our incipient star moved to the mike to begin his song, he glanced down at his friend and smiled confidently. Instead of returning the smile, his friend looked panic-stricken and mouthed these words, "Your fly is open!"

It was a moment of stark terror as *DISTRACTORS UNLIMITED* went to work on our singer's mind. First, there was the *EXTERNAL DISTRACTOR:* A so-called friend making frantic gestures about an embar-

rassing omission. This resulted in a host of *INTERNAL DISTRACTORS.* That small voice inside that once oozed with confidence now bellowed messages such as "You're going to blow this big chance" or "You look like a fool."

And sure enough, their combined efforts produced a complete shambles. He missed the meter of his opening notes, forgot the lyrics and was even afraid to include his usually smooth gestures for fear of displaying an ill-chosen, brightly hued pair of shorts. It was months before he was able to live down the fiasco, and his agent was able to explain away the situation and secure another booking that resumed his climb to the top.

We'll deal with *EXTERNAL DISTRACTORS* shortly, but right now, let's cup our shell-like ears to the *INTERNAL DISTRACTORS.*

All of us have gone through similar experiences, although probably with not so much at stake. You might meet a fantastic new guy; and a small voice in your head will say, "You'll probably say something stupid, and he won't ask you for a date." Or, you go into a classroom to take a final; and the voice says, "You're not prepared. You're probably going to flunk." Or, you're headed for a touchdown, and that miserable voice says, "You're probably going to drop the pass."

But luckily, there is another side to the coin. You can remember when you had great confidence in yourself and in your ability to deal with whatever happened. You feel that most of your friends and associates think highly of you, that most of what you attempt will succeed, and, if not, then it matters little. These are the times when that inner voice consistently is telling you how well you are doing and how much control you have. And usually, at these times, the voice is right.

These are examples of positive and negative self-talk. They represent a kind of continual feed-back that you use to monitor how you are doing and feeling.

Remember, back in Chapter 1, we saw that much of your mental activity is not verbal, but depends on feelings, sensations, impressions, and images. And one of the *TALKER's* favorite activities is to monitor these feelings or images and interpret them verbally. Your head hurts, and the *TALKER* will say, "Wow, what a miserable headache."

These feelings or images (and your verbal interpretations of them) determine to a great extent the "tone" of your world — whether it's good, bad or indifferent.

Marvelous, Fenker. That should go down with the discovery that standing near a fire causes you to be warm. Of course, my feelings influence my outlook on the world. And, I turn that into words. So what?

So this: We're describing only one-half of a two-way communication system. On the one hand, we can translate feelings into statements about how we're doing. But, on the other hand — and this is the most important fact — we can change how we feel by what we say to ourselves.

Let me repeat that: I said you can translate feelings into statements about how you're doing. But — and here's the point — we can also initiate verbal statements and use these suggestions to change our feelings!

"Every day in every way I'm getting better and better." I have those memorable words ironed on a cheap T-shirt in Day-Glo orange letters.

Well, even if that is a bit simplistic, it's not too far off the mark. What we're talking about here are two things:

1. The process of making appropriate suggestions to yourself in order to influence how you feel, and
2. Learning how to reach that state of mind in which the suggestions are most effective.

You are constantly being bombarded with feelings about your physical and mental states. Some of these are positive, some negative. The positive ones are no problem. To be a good learner, however, you must learn to deal effectively with the negative feelings. You must learn to change them to suit your purpose, to reduce anxiety, to eliminate unwanted distractions or to improve your self image.

SHHHH!

We call any form of negative self-talk an *INTERNAL DISTRACTOR.* These include not only negative statements about yourself, but also the interruptions or conflicts the *TALKER* can produce. *INTERNAL DISTRACTORS* represent a type of noise or confusion inside your head that interferes with most activities, especially learning. In order to learn effectively, your mind must be quiet and receptive or at least controlled.

—There are several kinds of negative self-

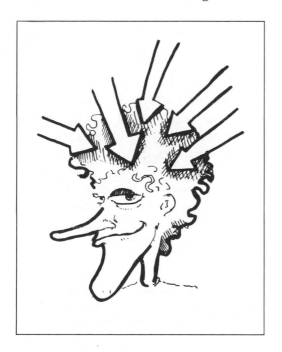

talk. Anxiety producing: you are unprepared and will flunk the exam. Defeatist: you've always fallen down on this ski run, and you will fall again this time. Distracting: I need to finish this chapter, but wow, what a great time I had dancing with Sam last night. All of these comments hinder learning in subtle, but devastating ways.

Let me tell you about Fenker's Foremost Frustration. For the past few years, I have offered a special class for beginning college students in learning to learn. Imagine, with my marvelous self-image, how shocked I was to find that I wasn't getting the job done. The students who might have benefited most from the class learned little or nothing! These were the one-third of the students who were having difficulty in most of their classes and who had little knowledge of learning methods or strategies.

Well, now, Fenker, you finally admit you can't really walk on water.

True, Nurf. I sank up to my naval on this one. It was difficult to understand, too. I considered the materials simple and almost self-explanatory. The class exercises were very basic, plus I gave considerable individual attention.

It took a number of follow-up interviews and questionnaires and many nights of worrying to find the answer. I had overlooked one vital fact: A poor repertoire of learning skills hinders the process of learning, slows it and makes it inefficient. But, it does not prevent learning from occurring. Regardless of the quality of a student's learning style, after 11 or 12 years experience, she can usually apply it well enough to get by, even in college.

But there are internal and external conditions which combine to prevent the process from ever being started, and even if it does start, they can prevent it from being continued effectively.[1]

The point I want to make here is that a learner must be able to cope with *INTERNAL* and *EXTERNAL DISTRACTORS* before she can start learning. This control is a basic necessity before specific strategies for memory and comprehension can be learned and successfully applied.

Remember that the *LISTENER* and the *TALKER* form a two-way communication system. The *TALKER* attempts to describe what the *LISTENER* is sensing or feeling. Thus, the content of your self-talk is heavily influenced by your feelings.

I have a feeling that we came by this way before. Or, is there an echo in here?

I repeat only to emphasize this point: You generate self-talk messages, which instead of reflecting your feelings, are intended to control them. In other words, what you tell yourself can change what you're feeling!

War between the states

Now, before we try to cure the problem, let's look at the symptoms. Most *INTERNAL DISTRACTORS* result from a conflict between what the *LISTENER* is feeling and what the *TALKER* is saying. For example, have you ever been reading a book (perhaps this book)[1] and noticed that you were reading the same page for the umpteenth time? When you start on the umpteenth-plus-one reading, that small inner voice immediately directs your attention to more important matters.

What is the *TALKER* saying? Probably that you are "supposed" (according to someone's plan) to read and understand the book. When you finish a page and don't understand what you have read, your self-talk instructs you to start over again.

What about the *LISTENER?* Clearly, the *LISTENER* is "feeling" that it would prefer some other activity. And, it is continually pulling at your mind with memories, day dreams, anxieties, plans, emotions and perhaps even sleep.

Thus, it may be very unrealistic and a waste of time to pick up a difficult textbook and simply begin reading. Why? The reason is this. "Reading" by itself is usual-

---

[1]You'll find documentation in Dr. Fenker's great unpublished work entitled "How I learned about why those who wanted to learn but couldn't learn because I hadn't learned how they could learn about learning." It was turned down by 84 publishers. (See *Guiness Book of Records.*)

[1]Especially this book!

ly not an effective method for learning difficult materials. And your mind protests this inappropriate activity by sending you signals that create feelings of boredom, frustration and dislike, as well as producing distracting images and self-talk.

If it feels bad, don't do it

These symptoms indicate you're probably using the wrong learning strategy, and they are a warning that you're involved in an unproductive effort. They are blowing the whistle on a fruitless activity and urging that you do something different. In a moment we'll take up techniques that will help reduce such *INTERNAL DISTRACTORS* and set you on a more profitable course.

Often, the conflicts between the *LISTENER* and the *TALKER* go far beyond problems associated with how or what you are learning. These more serious problems depend on emotional issues that affect both states of mind. Here are some examples you may recognize:

1. Frustration at not understanding.
2. Anxiety over examinations, papers, job assignments, a performance, a speech, an athletic event, etc.
3. Happiness or unhappiness about your relationship with a dating partner.
4. Anger at a friend, a teacher or parents.
5. Pressure from parents or friends.
6. Self-pity, self-hate, insecurity.
7. Fearing or dreading the consequence of some action.

You omitted the most pervasive fear of all Americans — that of going to a free, pay toilet with no money, shutting the door and finding the coin slot on the inside.

At times, Nurf, you make me feel as though I do slipshod work. But in any case, the *LISTENER's* feelings can disrupt the *TALKER's* attempt to study. Also, this process can work both ways. Most people are able to rationalize away feelings. "I should write the folks tonight." And they do it by using the *TALKER's* logic. "I'm too busy tonight, I'll wait until tomorrow."

In both cases, it produces a conflict between two states of mind — a feeling, sensing state and a verbal, logical state. And it is this battle that generates the *INTERNAL DISTRACTORS* which intrude on the learning process.

Getting control without whip or chair

Control of *INTERNAL DISTRACTORS* depends on balancing or harmonizing both states. How? Well, assume you're reading, and your concentration is interrupted by strong feelings of anxiety about getting a poor grade. One way to achieve balance is for the *TALKER* to ask the *LISTENER* to take away these feelings, to postpone them or to neutralize them in some way.

Try this:

> "The math exam is over. I know I did poorly, but I can't change the fact by worrying. It's important now for me to do well on my English test tomorrow. Therefore, I want to get rid of all feelings of upset, self-dislike and anxiety. I want my entire mind to be relaxed, but also aware and able to concentrate fully on these English stories."

And remember, too, a self-talk program has maximum effect when you are in a relaxed or meditative state.

Other problems can't be banished in an instant. These are the ones that build up over many months or years. They might include test anxiety, general unhappiness, lack of confidence, fear of failure or a "broken heart." Self-talk programs are very useful in treating such problems if (1) you recognize that resolution of the problem will require time and (2) the temporary benefits can be noticed and appreciated immediately, although the problem has not yet disappeared.

You're not alone

If your self-talk seems to be weighted on the negative side, don't consider yourself unique. Each semester I have my students monitor their self-talk. My statistics (admittedly a bit crude) show that about 60 percent of these students have more negative self-talk than they do neutral or positive self-talk. And further, if I separate out the students having learning problems, then 80 percent to 90 percent of them have self-talk that is predominantly negative. I believe this is extremely significant.

How about you? Well, there's one way to find out. Here's what I want you to do: Spend a few days actually listening to the messages you're sending to yourself.

If your messages are largely negative, make a list of them and try to substitute neutral or positive statements in their place. What you tell yourself as a learner affects the way you perform. If your self-talk is over-critical, you won't enjoy trying to learn. Negative statements interfere with learning tasks. Thus, it is important to control them using right-brain states and substituting more positive self-talk.

I encourage my students, when they are in a right-brain state, to imagine themselves overcoming any problems. Gary, who suffers from test anxiety, is asked to imagine himself feeling relaxed and confident as he takes an up-coming exam. Shirley, who has a fear of public speaking, is asked to imagine herself giving a report in front of a class.

I can just see them — lying there together, playing with their right brains. They'll both end up with zits.

Sorry, Nurf, but it works, the combination of the relaxed state and the positive message. But, it also works when you're in a normal, active left-brain state. Thus, if your self-talk continually reminds you that you're tired, upset, anxious, happy, good, bad, stupid, etc., you probably will have feelings to match.

Then, instead of saying "I think; therefore, I am," we should say, "I am what I think." Personally, I am mostly what I eat.

That's close Nurf, but in your case it's what you drink, not what you eat that matters. Since each problem requires a unique solution, here's Fenker's Tremendous Trio that may serve as useful models for developing your own messages.

1. **Relaxation break between study periods** — While I am relaxed I will remove all feelings of tiredness from my body and mind. When I return to study, I will be able to concentrate fully on my work. My mind and senses will be keen and alert. When I awaken, I will feel full of energy and will apply that energy to my learning tasks.

2. **Personal problem with teacher, date, etc.** — While I am relaxed I will consider my problems with the teacher (Dr. Trafney Grunge). I will imagine a picture of Dr. Grunge and myself. In that image, I see strong darts or feelings of dislike, distrust or anxiety radiating toward Dr. Grunge and also surrounding him. I realize that before I can expect Dr. Grunge to act differently toward me, I must change my negative feelings about him. I will see these feelings of dislike gradually disappear. I will not let those negative feelings dominate my perception. Dr. Grunge's feelings no longer disturb me. They are his problem, not my own.

3. **Negative attitude toward learning abilities** — While I am relaxed, I will focus on my problems as a learner. I am not as effective a learner as I would like to be. My present level of effectiveness does not matter and need cause me no further concern. This level is simply where I am today. I will not blame myself, feel

bad or regret where I am today. I simply accept this as a given fact.

What matters is that I start at this point and begin to improve. When I wake up from this relaxed state, I will find that improvement has already started. I will feel full of energy, alert and ready to concentrate on my learning tasks. I can imagine a picture of my head and see all of the negative feelings about myself bombarding it. Now, I'll simply turn those feelings around so they radiate outward, instead of inward. Eventually, they will disappear. Each day when I relax, I will find that I am a better and better learner until there are no negative feelings to turn away.

Not bad, Fenker. I am now alert, energetic, on my way to being a better learner, able to leap small buildings in a single bound. And, I'm afraid I'm falling in love with Dr. Grunge.

He's married, Nurf. Don't break up a happy home.

Chapter 4

Dealing With External Distractors

How Sex, TV, Pizza and Beer Can Help You Study

You'll probably recall that in the Introduction[1] . . . Okay, you don't recall. But I did compare learning to taking a trip. So let's take one.

In preparation for the trip, you've mastered the skills offered in the last chapter (although this normally will require at least several weeks of practice). Thus, your travel vehicle, whether a beat up Volkswagen or a shining Ferrari, is internally sound. Your learning trip is underway, and you're looking out of both windows. Ah, ha, there's a brilliant billboard which grabs your attention. It warns: "EDI Crossing Ahead." Your eyes fixiate on the sign, and you barely miss a large truck.

Next, there appears a roadside cafe advertising "The World's Largest Earthworm in Captivity." You just can't miss this, so you pull off and stop for a half-an-hour. Your learning trip is temporarily halted.

Well, that was a mistake. The worm turns out to be a snake dressed in a nylon body stocking. And, as you leave, you notice a small sign. The legend: "Sponsored by EDI."

Back on the road for a while and another road sign looms: "Scenic Detour Ahead. For only a short delay, you can experience sensational sights." Again, in small letters at the bottom of the sign are the initials "EDI."

But you're a sucker and can't resist. What's an hour when you can see Funky Gorge, the Incomplete Mountains and the River of No Mystery?

Sights seen, back on the road, you yawn, check your watch and pull into a motel. When you examine your map, you're amazed to find that you're only a couple of miles from where you started.

What happened? Instead of following a straight route, you allowed your learning trip to be controlled by that fiendish organization, "External Distractors, Incorporated." You may be more familiar with their subsidiaries — TV, records, pictures, friends' voices, the bed, your suitemate, a six-pack, and so forth. Your learning experience bombed because EDI had your attention most of the time instead of the materials you planned to learn enroute.

Fenker, that's a mighty strange allegory.

---

[1]No one needs introductions. See study by Glanders and Crupper — *"The Introduction, a Function of the Author's Ego."* In their introduction to this study, G. & C. point out that introductions serve as a receptacle for unused bookmarks, gasoline receipts, strips of bacon and letters from home.

That was no allegory, Nurf. That was a lizard in a body stocking. But, the point I want to make is that it wouldn't have mattered whether you were in a Volkswagen or a Ferrari. (We're assuming, of course, the Ferrari was loaded with all of the learning techniques offered in this book, while the Volkswagen was not.) Your trip would still have been a dismal failure unless you somehow learned to deal effectively with EDI.

In order to master new learning techniques, it will be necessary for you to improve your behavioral or self-control skills. It's not enough to offer you a smorgas-board of high-powered study techniques and say, "Here, take what you need." Until you have mastered some crucial behavioral skills, it's doubtful you can effectively use the learning techniques offered in later chapters. And that's why we are dealing with distractors and self-control problems at this point in the book.

What is an *EXTERNAL DISTRACTOR?* From the examples I just gave, it's obvious they are such things as interesting sounds, pictures, people or activities — those things that draw your attention away from a learning task. They include anything external to the learner that serves to distract him from his intended focus. The obvious ones, such as TV, people talking or beer in the refrigerator, can be dealt with in a straightforward manner. You simply shut off the TV, get away from the people or keep the refrigerator closed.

More devastating, however, are the *EXTERNAL DISTRACTORS* you build into your learning style. Yes, YOU!! As a rule, they're not only well disguised, but often they are extremely difficult to eliminate because they can change form, or they can adapt as you develop new learning skills.

Habits can be habit forming

Take, for example, some subtle distractors — coffee, cigarettes or Cokes. If you find you're taking breaks every few minutes to enjoy one of these reinforcers, then perhaps you have developed a habit. These things are not necessarily bad, per se. But if they've been associated with learning or studying for a period of time, then in effect, you have "built in" a distractor as part of your learning activities.

Now, they may be excellent rewards; but they should not be included as part of your learning style. And, the reason is simple: They direct your attention towards activities which are incompatible with learning.

To increase your efficiency as a learner, one goal is particularly important: the elimination of all behavior incompatible with learning. For, as long as these behaviors commonly take place during study, they compete for your attention

with proper learning behaviors. If you're a chain smoker or a constant coffee guzzler, try this: Study intensely for a short period, even if it's only five minutes. Then, use the cigarette as a reward for concentrating during that period. But, don't do both activities at the same time.

Let's take another type of distractor — a habit pattern that is counter-productive. Many students do everything at the last minute. They put off all assignments until the end of the term, they cram for exams, they write papers only hours before the deadline. And in fact, this strategy often pays off since it produces maximum benefits (adequate grades) for minimum time and effort.

Yet, this pattern cannot work well for all activities. You must give daily attention to such tasks as learning new concepts, researching a problem or mastering a foreign language.

Other assignments requiring constant attention include those associated with cumulative learning such as mathematics or physics. In these areas, you start with simple principles and problems which get steadily more complicated by building on what was previously learned. In the short run, a deadline strategy may work well, but if it becomes a habit, it will probably interfere with your attempts to learn systematically.

Thus, it's obvious that students can become locked-in on a strategy controlled by a certain set of external conditions — in this case, a deadline. It would be much better, however, if the nature of the task itself — studying for an exam, learning a language, solving problems — determined whether a last-minute deadline approach or a systematic approach is more appropriate.

Me? I prefer a deadline approach on any task that fits the description of "busy work." Such a job doesn't require a great deal of thought — just the time and effort to sit down and finish it. Large tasks requiring much time, thought or creativity, I break up and treat piece-by-piece in a systematic manner.

Fenker, I am a Coke fiend. Also, I always wait until the last minute; but I don't consider those my best points. What I am proudest of is my ability to look at an assignment, especially an important one, and then walk away from it. That takes character!

It may also take the price of a ticket back home from college. Some of us weirdo academicians don't take kindly to blank paper or empty seats.

But you're right. The most common habit which causes students problems (and teachers, too) is the simple avoidance of study or academic work. I'm sure you've developed some elaborate techniques and rationales for not doing what you know you have to do. Try these on and see if they sound familiar:

1. I'm too tired to study now.
2. I'll be more effective tomorrow, tomorrow night, Sunday afternoon, St. Swithin's Day, etc.
3. No sense starting this paper until I have all the reference materials at hand.
4. (males) I'll study as soon as I call Aureola.
5. (females) I'll study as soon as I call Ronnie Baby.

Such excuses are major distractors. Why? Because they allow us to do the things we like better than studying. They are substitutes for genuine learning behaviors. And we continue to do them because they're the easy way out.

Too often, we make decisions primarily on the basis of whether or not they will have immediate positive consequences or results. We want it today. Not tomorrow or next week or at the end of the term.

And this will continue until we do two things. One, we must accept responsibility for our actions, that is, admit that we are at fault. And two, we must genuinely want to change.

Let's take a couple of distractors. "I'm often disturbed by my roommate's loud radio" and "I can never get started to work quickly." It may seem they are quite different. The first involves a single distractor that can be eliminated by turning off the radio. The second involves changing a complex habit pattern. But in truth, both are associated with behaviors that occur frequently enough to be habits.

Not starting to work is clearly your problem. But, so is the noisy radio. If it has occurred a number of times, wasn't it your responsibility to turn it off or speak to your roommate about it?

Perhaps you have let it become a reinforcement for a bad habit. What a marvelous excuse it is for not being able to study well or not receiving good grades. It's easier to blame the radio than to admit that you're really at fault.

If you're going to get personal, Fenker, I think I'll skip the rest of this chapter. There's something in the Constitution that protects us from the invasion of privacy.

Come on, Nurf, don't play the Prince of Paranoia. It is your responsibility, and if you want to change, you'll have to accept it.

Now, the question is: do you really want to change? If you do, you must make it unrewarding to do the things that are a substitute for learning.

Look, Fenker, there's no way you're going to tell me that beating my brains out is more rewarding than not beating my brains out. How much can I get turned on by memorizing the names and middle initials of the 24 Court Chamberlains during the reign of Huckbald the Fat?

I didn't say you would. There'll always be assignments and subjects you don't

like. But while avoiding them is a kind of reward, it's short-lived; and down the road, you're going to be in big trouble with your exams and grades.

So the answer is this: You substitute another type of reward. And that is the reward of efficient learning — spending as little time as possible and still doing well on exams.

If you really want to eliminate these distractors, you must accept the goal of learning efficiently instead of the goal of avoiding these unpleasant tasks.

If you go for the immediate reward of a short term goal — getting out of studying — at the expense of the long term goal — getting a good grade — the result is conflict and frustration. And I've seen this get so bad with some students, they were incapable of studying anything.

Let me use you, Nurf, as a guinea pig. What did you do last night when it came time to hit the books?

Well, I got my books out and started reading. Then I heard these characters out in the second floor lounge talking, so I took a short break to find out what was going on and ended up with Aureola and . . .

Thanks, Nurf. That's enough. You see, real conflict. Your long term goal was getting an "A" in history: Your short term goal was seeing Aureola.

I need attention.

The problem with long term goals (and the reason they are called "long term") is that the things you do to attain them — such as studying — have no immediate positive consequences. Short term goals by definition have rewards that are almost immediate. And when you're faced with the choice of studying history or seeing Aureola, the opportunity for immediate gratification often controls what you do.

Let's take Nurf's problem and look at it more carefully. His long term goal is to get an "A" in history. What does it take, Nurf?

Bribing my teacher? Well, it probably would take studying at least five days a week.

Okay, we'll buy that. Studying is necessary to reach your long range goal. Now, what about the short range goal? In your case, the answer is obvious. You simply walk outside to Aureola's van which is al-

ways parked right outside your dorm.

Now, let's look at the consequences of these two actions — first studying.

Pluses

1. You're current on assignments.
2. You're on track for the semester.
3. You're free of anxiety and guilt.
4. You feel good about your accomplishment.

Minuses

1. You don't see Aureola.
2. You have to work.

Now, let's go see Aureola.

Pluses

1. You're with Aureola.

Minuses

1. You're falling behind in history.
2. You're not prepared for class.
3. You're filled with guilt and anxiety.
4. You're going to have to do the work sometime or blow the course.

Convinced? Well, the truth is that except for feeling good about completing the assignment or being free of guilt, there's nothing in the plus column for studying that has an immediate reward value. And when you balance the possibility of feeling good against the sure thing of being with Aureola, it's easy to see why Nurf cops out for the short term goal.

What's the answer? Clearly, motivation is one key. You do have to have a genuine desire to learn history well enough to get an "A." This book and its techniques can't replace that critical motivation. On the other hand, you can be sincere in your desire to learn, but need help. And that's what ol' Fenker can offer.

Let's summarize the problem.

LONG TERM GOAL: get an "A"
BEHAVIOR REQUIRED: study history regularly

SHORT TERM GOAL: be with Aureola
BEHAVIOR REQUIRED: walk to her van

CONFLICT: Nurf prefers behavior with immediate consequences (being with Aureola) to behavior necessary to get an "A" (studying)
SOLUTION: Connect the desired behavior of studying with immediate positive consequences.

Sound impossible? Well, if you really don't care, it is. But, if you have a genuine desire to get an "A" and you're willing to accept the responsibility for your actions, here's how:

Fanfare[1]

---

[1]Tah-ta-ta-tah-ta-ta-ta-dah!

Introducing Fenker's Stupendous System for Study Management!

Objective: to identify and reinforce those learning behaviors necessary to accomplish long range goals (while keeping the van in sight).

Plan your system

1. Determine what's wrong now. Outline the whole array of behaviors connected with your learning activities. What are your long and short range goals? What positive or negative reinforcers are connected with each? What are you doing to get an immediate reward at the expense of achieving long term objectives?

2. State your goals clearly. Don't say, "I want to do better." That's meaningless. When you state your goals in vague terms, you can always rationalize your way to success regardless of what is actually accomplished. Instead, say, "I want to study two hours a night," or "I want to complete each math assignment on time." Make your objectives specific enough to be counted, measured and observed.

3. Think small. Start with objectives small enough to be accomplished. You can always expand them as

you get your system in operation.

4. Be realistic. Your system must be able to function in the real world. Promising yourself a trip to Tahiti for passing an exam just isn't in the cards.

Designing your system

Your objective is to create a system which allows a difficult activity such as studying to compete successfully with your other short term goals. To do this, you must learn to use rewards or punishments to focus your learning activities on your long range goals. Here are a few of the tools you have to work with:

1. Positive reinforcement: Give yourself a reward for completing a small task or assignment. It might be pizza, beer, a TV program or a movie. Study two hours and collect.

2. Negative reinforcement: Rewards may not be enough. A Coke might not be enough motivation to study for two hours, so add a negative reinforcer. If you don't complete your behavioral objective, deny yourself dessert or limit the money you can spend on a certain activity. Or you can remove the positive reinforcer — no bull session if you sluff off the math assignment.

3. Premack principle: Don't let the name scare you off. It can be used when you simply run out of positive or negative reinforcers. (You may just get sick of Cokes.) It says that behavior which occurs frequently is more reinforcing than behavior which occurs less frequently. What do you do a lot? Eat? Get in bull sessions? Needle point? Work on your car? Gab on the phone? It's easy to apply this principle. Just make a deal with yourself that until you complete the task or assignment, you won't engage in these high frequency behaviors.

Implement the system.

Try it. See if it works. And don't make exceptions or change it unless you're willing to start all over. You'll find that devilish little demon in your head is continually trying to disrupt your system. You're tired. You need that Coke now. Forty-five minutes of study instead of an hour is enough. If you don't finish the paper on time, you're supposed to cut your fun-money by two bucks . . . but what the hell — you only live once.
Take that little demon by the throat and shake him firmly.

Fenker, get your hands off my body.

Quiet, Nurf. Just make no exceptions, and his voice will become softer and less convincing.

Fenker's Soap Opera: "All My Students"

Jeff[1] — Jeff was as a pushover for distractors — his record player, his girlfriend's picture, voices in the hall, thoughts about eating. They all operated to prevent him from starting to study and kept his attention span limited to only a few minutes once he had begun. He loved bull sessions and would be up until all hours every night talking with friends.

Here's what Jeff did. First, he eliminated the obvious distractors — the record player and the picture — from the study area. He established this contingency: he would study effectively for two hours each evening before he could get into a bull session. And, only productive time could count toward the total two hours.

In the first week, Jeff reported it was hard to stay with the system. Since he was continually distracted, the two hours stretched into three and four very quickly. But after the second week, he found he was usually through studying around eight o'clock and was beginning to feel very good about some of the classes he had previously disliked. Jeff later received his masters degree and appeared on the "Gong Show."

Evaluate your system.

If it's working, leave it alone. If it's not, start over. Redo your analysis and find out why. Then, put together another system you believe will work.

Remember, much of your present behavior is regulated by just such systems. With these processes outlined, you can gain awareness and insight into the mechanics of the system and so regulate them to replace old bad habits with new effective ones.

Let me tell you about some of the people I've worked with and how they solved their problems this way.

---

[1]Dr. Fenker has purposely identified them by their real names because he has a nasty desire to embarrass the hell out of them.

Mary — She hated to study French with a passion.[1] But two semesters of language were required for her Fine Arts degree. On the other hand, she loved English Literature and could read novels for hours. Simple solution: She would not allow herself to read any English Literature until she had studied French for at least an hour. She reported no problems with this system. She doesn't like French any better than before, but she finds she has usually completed her French assignment before dinner so her evenings will be free for more pleasant activities. She also had her teeth fixed, got rid of her pimples and inherited more than a $100,000 from an aunt she had never heard of.

Ralph — The greatest procrastinator of them all. He did all right in some cases by waiting until the last minute. But he had great difficulty with term papers and other major projects. These were typically turned in late and were often down-graded. We failed in our attempts to use various positive rewards as incentives to study on a daily basis. Part of the problem was that beer and records were things Ralph had always had in excess and hence were taken so much for granted, they didn't work well as rewards.

We finally set up a negative reinforcement system oriented around his chopped, channeled and whatevered muscle car. When a term paper was assigned, he wrote out a day-by-day schedule covering the period until it was due. We set up small goals, as little as 15 to 20 minutes of preparatory work per day. If he didn't complete the day's schedule, his roommate got the car keys and held them for the evening. Surprisingly, this system seemed to work pretty well, without sacrificing the roommate's friendship. Ralph's car was later stolen and stripped. He was last seen sitting in the bare frame writing an essay.

Betty — She exhibited Fenker's Famous Food/Tube Syndrome. She was extremely overweight and cut classes right and left to watch daytime TV. And she continued on through the evening, sitting in front of the set surrounded by candy, chips, and Cokes, instead of studying.

We tackled her problem in stages. First, we tried to separate her eating behavior from her television watching. She could continue to snack when she wanted, but she wasn't allowed to eat or drink while she was watching the tube. This seemed to work fairly well. She cut down

---

[1]She also hated to study French without a passion which seemed to exhaust her emotional range.

her intake tremendously, and she even began to lose a little weight.

Next, we moved to bring TV watching under control. We established a system where, if she missed a single class, she could not watch daytime television for the day. She stuck to her guns and after missing one or two classes, she did deny herself the TV watching. Within a week she was attending all classes.

Last, we set a goal of two hours of study outside of class each day. And we established a contingency that this study must be completed before any television could be watched. In a

short time, she was not only attending classes, but studying during the afternoons so her evenings would be free for TV. When the term ended, she received quite high grades, and to my surprise, over the summer she lost almost 30 pounds. (I honestly don't know what system she followed to do this.)

Betty was discovered by a Hollywood producer and changed her name to Farrah Familiar and was never heard of again.

Look, Fenker, I'll believe everything about the pimples and inheritance, the stolen car and the Hollywood producer, but you'll never convince me these cats learned to study and get better grades. I'm not that naïve.

Sorry, Nurf. These are true behavioral management stories. And I included them because they were successful. They worked because the students were serious about changing their behavior. They developed reasonable systems and stuck to them. And their reward was improved learning behavior. Many other students in my classes developed systems that didn't work. (And, if you think I'm going to tell you about them, you're crazy.) In some cases the systems were at fault — the rewards inadequate or too far off, or the goals and consequences were not clearly stated. But the most common reason for failure was that the students didn't stick to the rules they had established. That's why we insist that you follow your system to the letter or forget it.

Don't fight the system

Before shutting down on this chapter, I want to return to one problem mentioned earlier — the "last minute" or "deadline" syndrome. Putting off things until the last minute is a popular study style in high school and college. This syndrome involves cramming the night before the exam, writing papers at the last minute, not keeping up with daily assignments and needing deadlines to complete any work. Most books on learning stress that this syndrome is bad and represents an ineffective method of learning.

This is not necessarily true. If such strategies were that bad or inefficient, students would soon catch on and not use them. But, instead they're employed by both good and bad students. I believe this reflects something important about the way contingency systems operate in many schools. For, in some respects, the system rewards such last minute approaches to learning.

How? Well, there are at least two ways:
1. By giving exams that focus on the recall of material that can simply be memorized, rather than more conceptual material that takes time to comprehend, and
2. By structuring class activities so students don't have adequate incentives for keeping up or studying the material on a regular basis.

Most students are incredibly sophisticated at choosing work strategies that will minimize their efforts for a given long term goal — whether that goal is simply to pass or get an "A." If it is perceived as less time-consuming to adopt a last minute approach AND if the system rewards this approach, clearly students will continue to use it.

The use of a deadline system is just fine in many cases. But it's important to separate those classes and activities in which last minute strategies will succeed from those in which they will not. Deadline strategies will seem to be efficient for courses that are primarily memorization-oriented and for some kinds of writing such as free-style papers. However, research work, conceptual learning and most creative and problem solving activities require time. Period.[1]

---

[1] If this chapter seems to end somewhat abruptly, you're right. Dr. Fenker stopped writing and went over to the faculty lounge where he was last seen with a package of Cheezits, a Coke and a long cigar, watching "Days of Our Lives" on the tube. He plans to finish this chapter the night before it is scheduled to be mailed to the publisher. We all wish him well in his efforts to complete it before the deadline because it would . . .

Chapter 5

Monitoring Your Learning Behavior

Hungry for Knowledge? Then Put on the Old Feedback

If your grade and high school teachers had used the same methods to teach you to drive as they did to teach you to learn, you would be a class of tender-footed pedestrians. And a trip on the freeway would make a demolition derby seem tame by comparison.

Way to go, Fenker. Now attack your fellow educators. Why, if you're not careful, they will drum you out of that ivory-covered office and use all those funny diplomas to carpet their birdcages.

I'll risk it, Nurf. Let's look at driving a car. It's a complicated task. You must learn to coordinate the movement of the wheel with that of the brakes, clutch and accelerator. You've got to be constantly monitoring the condition of the road, the presence of other cars, the instruments on the dash and the boyfriend or girlfriend sitting next to you, who can be very distracting.

And yet, millions of people learn to become highly skilled drivers each year after only a few months of practice. Also, more experienced drivers can coordinate all of the above actions intuitively, without conscious effort, at the same time they are eating, talking or smoking.

I can hear in my mind's ear a multitude of you chorusing, "Prithee, Dr. Fenker, how can such a complicated skill be learned so quickly and so well that it becomes automatic for almost anyone?"

Well, gather 'round for I'm about to share a Fenker Fundamental: Constant Feedback.

During the process of learning, someone — a parent, friend or driving instructor — was continually providing feedback information. Remember? "You're going too fast; slow down. There's a stop sign at this intersection. Stay in your lane. Try not to hit that curb . . . again."

The road itself provides still more. On an uphill grade, the car begins to slow, telling you to push harder on the accelerator. If you drift onto the shoulder, the wheels start bumping and bouncing. Other drivers have their input also. Cross the center line, and the oncoming driver will blast his horn and scream some thoughtful analysis of your parentage and/or mental condition.

Virtually every incorrect action in an auto has some form of immediate feedback associated with it, including at some unfortunate times, the unattractive sound of bending metal.

But feedback is of limited value unless you are able to understand it and use it

49

properly. Most beginning drivers quickly develop "self-talk" programs based on their experiences or their friends' comments. And these programs become their bag of responses to situations which can occur — going on to the shoulder, reaching a hill, avoiding the animal at the "Dragon Crossing" sign.

In fact, the major difference between good and bad drivers is not physical ability. It is that good drivers have an appropriate collection of programs for responding to any situation likely to occur.

Consider what happens when you find yourself skidding on wet or icy roads. An effective self-talk program might include the messages, "Don't hit the brakes"; or, "Turn the wheels in the direction of the skid."

You can't be serious, Fenker. By the time you repeated this message in a real emergency, your car would be upside down in the ditch and the insurance claim already filed.

True, Nurf, for experienced drivers, most of these programs operate automatically at a subconscious level. Thus, the response is virtually instantaneous with little self-talk. However, most people rely a great deal on self-talk programs while they

are learning to drive. But, soon these programs become automatic.

My self-talk program is saying "All this jazz about driving is getting boring. Get to the point!"

Okay, learning to drive is in many respects like learning to learn — except for one major difference. When you learn to drive, the process of driving, how you operate the auto, is considered to be most important. Where you are going, your destination, is a minor concern. Why? Because, once you are skilled in the process, it's assumed you can drive anywhere you choose.

Unfortunately, in schools and colleges, the process of learning — how you go about learning something — is given secondary importance. The primary emphasis and hence, most of the feedback, concerns whether you reach a particular goal — passing an exam, remembering a list of names and dates, finishing a paper, solving a problem or receiving a diploma.

Imagine a driving instructor telling you, "Take me to Lost Truss, Wyoming,"[1] and then not commenting on how well you were driving but only on how long it took you to get there. You may have wandered all over the road, broken the speed-

---

[1] I'm sure you readers are curious about Lost Truss, Wyoming. Well, it's so small — now get this — it's so small that the words "City Limits" and "Resume Speed" are painted on the same sign.

EDITOR'S NOTE: Gorbish will be out for a few pages while we run a check on his "humor" circuits.

laws, ignored every good driving practice known to man, but not have received any feedback!

To become skilled at driving or learning, you need to develop self-talk programs that monitor how well or how poorly you are performing these activities. I call these special self-talk routines *SELF-MONITORING PROGRAMS.*

In order to make a significant improvement in your learning skills, you must develop programs comparable to those of very effective learners. Using these programs will guide and shape your learning behavior until much of the process becomes automatic like eating, walking or driving.

Now, let's get into the origin of self-monitoring programs, how such programs influence learning and how you can develop programs suitable for your learning style.

Who says what, when

Let's review how a self-talk program works . . . who talks, who listens and to what purpose. Much of your conscious activity consists of a constant stream of messages from the *TALKER* about the world and how you are functioning in it. Most people carry a kind of "model" of the world around in their heads. This model, which is based largely on our successes and failures, represents what we think is likely to occur or not occur in any situation. Gradually, those programs which relate to physical activities will be-

come non-conversational and intuitive. But programs related to mental activities or decisions may remain conversational indefinitely. "I think I'll wear the beige tank top to the inauguration. No, maybe the one with the puce stripes will look better." Or, they may also become intuitive. "I don't know anything about art, but I know what I like."

Who writes the script?

Self-talk programs about learning come from many sources — elementary school teachers, parents, television and finally, trial and error testing of your own. Only a few grade schools and high schools offer formal training in learning skills. The result is that many students in high school or entering college have self-monitoring programs that are as likely to impede effective learning as they are to encourage it. Take for example this scenario.

A clever high school student, Jane Smart, has that old problem we discussed in the last chapter. She has found she can do well with only a little last minute studying. Her self-talk might go like this: "I don't feel like working right now, but no matter, I can always do it later." And that's where her trouble begins.

It's hard to break this habit, because it rewards her not just once, but twice. First, it works (sort of). Jane can wait until the last minute and still get adequate grades on papers and exams. Second, she has an immediate reward for putting off studying. She can now eat, watch TV, talk to

STOP STUDYING: START LEARNING

friends, or whatever. And even though such self-monitoring programs result in disaster in some classes, they are hard to change because they may continue to succeed in others.

In my classes, I have watched many students get into trouble trying to open college doors with a set of crude learning keys, fashioned earlier in grade school or high school. And, surprisingly, they will persist in this practice, despite the fact that most of them do understand more effective learning habits. They have mastered the content of learning strategies, but have not put them into practice even though they recognize the need for change.

What might help these students? Well, on paper it's simple. they need to develop self-monitoring programs that will encourage, not hinder the application of effective learning strategies. These become a set of built-in controls.[1] In fact, I'll make you the following promise.

A Money-Back Guarantee

You can drastically improve your ability to learn by simply learning how to monitor your learning activities! Why? Because the quality of all conscious activity depends largely on the quality of the related self-monitoring programs. And when you

are studying, it is these programs which determine the sequence of thoughts and actions you execute while reading, writing or problem solving.

How do monitoring programs work? They provide the feedback necessary to change or correct what you are doing. For example, in basketball if all your shots were falling short of the basket, a good self-talk program might say, "Shoot harder, dummy!" In learning tasks, your programs should operate to keep your mind actively engaged.

How important are such programs? If you stop reading after this chapter and toss the book in trash,[2] you could still make a dramatic change in your learning ability by using the self-monitoring programs described below.

How to fold Tab "A" into slot "B"

Now, we're going to build a self-monitoring program. And, the easiest way to do it is to model your program after a good learner. Why not? They have programs which work. Let's start by tuning in on Nurf's head again, after he has tried to read a chapter in a fairly difficult philosophy book.

"It's eleven o'clock, and I still have

---

[1]Dr. Fenker is referring to a form of psychocybernetics or, in other words, a self-generated feedback/regulatory mechanism. You humans seem to have trouble developing such mechanisms. As a computer, of course, most of my logic circuits are precisely controlled by XRKL3 N$FLTRENT @EIOU EIEIO!

[2]Clearly, a foolish thing to do.

to read this junk. It's boring, and I'm exhausted. Well, let's get comfortable. (Opens book idly, flips through the pages, notes some interesting doodles he made during last week's classes) Hmmm. Wonder what that one was supposed to be. Looks like a bug-eyed owl. Well, I've read the first page, and it doesn't mean anything. Guess I'll read it again.

Man, it's warm in here. Epistemology. What the heck does that mean? Probably not important. Well, I'm at the bottom of the page again and still no sale. One more time. Esthetic beauty. Esthetic beauty. Aureola has esthetic beauty and a number of other things. Mind's wandering . . . Again."

(Thirty minutes and two pages later) "This is really tough stuff. But 45

minutes is long enough. A whole chapter of this is too much for one night. Aureola is probably showering her esthetic beauty about now. Wonder what that police siren means? Probably the campus flasher is making his rounds again."

Where did you get that transcript?[1] That's pretty close to what happened.

Okay, let's apply some effective self-monitoring programs to this situation.

options

1. "It's eleven o'clock, and I must read this chapter. It's tough, and I'm tired. So I won't study more than 30 minutes. I think I'll underline the major points I read. This will help me to stay awake and remember the material tomorrow.

2. "I couldn't make any sense out of the first page. I'll try to paraphrase it in my own words. At least it will help me ask some sensible questions in class tomorrow."

3. "My mind has wandered all through this first page. I know I'm tired, and this is rough material. It makes more sense to tackle something easier and more stimulating right now. I think I'll outline these English sentences

---

[1]By sending one dollar and a catfood label to Merkel Press.

instead and save the philosophy until tomorrow morning when I'm rested."

These are good programs because they monitor when you're getting off the track and suggest ways to get back on.

Time's A Wastin'

All self-monitoring programs focusing on learning should have one overriding goal: to insure that the time you intend to devote to learning is spent effectively.

In Nurf's case, a good program would have noted his tiredness and decided (a) that it would be a waste of time to continue, or (b) that 30 minutes of effective study was about the limit at this point of the evening. Then it would have concluded that he either fold up for the night or continue only for a short time.

Hold it, Fenker. It's not always that easy. Suppose I have a philosophy test the next day, and I simply can't afford to go to sleep. You want to tell my understanding professor the next morning that ol' Fenker's Magic Formula for Success instructed me to catch about eight hours of "Z's" and that I will be glad to drop around at another time to take his quaint, little exam?

Not at all. In your case, the "I must finish reading this before the test" program will take precedence over the "I'm wiped out" program. It makes little sense to read the pages over and over again without comprehension. So, your decision must incorporate both monitoring operations. You must relax or sleep before you try to study. Or you must decide to work for a period sufficiently brief for your concentration to be maintained.

In other words, in developing good self-monitoring programs, even when you're faced with several conflicting problems, don't select an irrational plan that only wastes your time. If you have to sleep or study for only a short time to be effective, do it.

Hew to the straight and narrow

Imagine yourself as a metal ball surrounded by magnets of different sizes. In the distance is the largest magnet representing your learning goal and toward which you're moving. Nearby are smaller magnets representing internal distractors such as being sleepy and external distractors such as your boyfriend's picture.

In Figure 5-1, your path can be devious, indirect and time consuming as the majority of your travel time is spent going perpendicular to your goal. You've permitted the distractors to draw your attention away from the goal. Figure 5-1 also shows how a good self-monitoring program works. Each time your attention is drawn away from your goal, a program immediately intervenes. It directs you to act in a way that gets you back on the track.

You'll note that in both instances, your

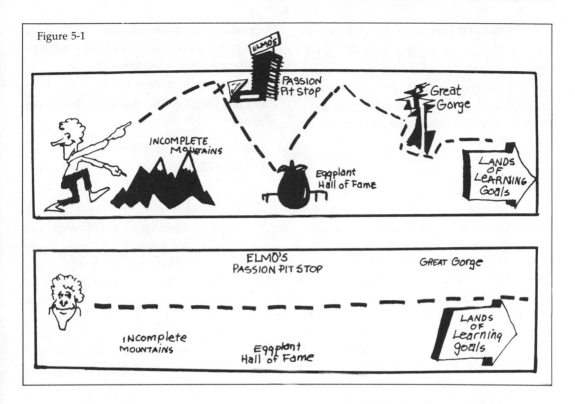

Figure 5-1

learning trip frequently changes direction. All learners, good and bad, are continually tempted away from the straight and narrow. But the best learners have self-monitoring programs that are continually noting these distractions, blowing the whistle and suggesting the proper corrective actions. The major difference in the two illustrations is the length of the deviation from the optimum course.

The poor learner reads the first page over and over, because each time, his mind has wandered to other subjects. When he reached the bottom of the page, his program asked: "Before you go on, did you understand what you've read?" The answer being "No," he mechanically began again at the top of the page. After repeating this several times, another part of the program said, "You've read this several times. This is really rough. Don't waste anymore time on it. Go on to the next page."

It's a program all right. But it was designed to insure only that some progress was made through the book. It did not guarantee that learning was occurring. The good learner, however, noted the problem quickly after only one reading of the page.

Little things can kill you.

The most important characteristic of all effective self-monitoring programs is this: they are designed to note small changes in your behavior or feelings and then to take action before the situation develops into a major problem.

What happened with the good learner? He was sensitive to those subtle clues that indicated he was off the track — drowsiness, distractions, procrastination, unrelated subjects, failing to understand a sentence. He immediately shifted to a more active form — from "reading" to "reading with paraphrasing." The good learner noted quickly when the material was too difficult to be studied effectively, so he almost immediately shifted to something else. Our poor learner had to be hit over the head with a two-by-four before he recognized the trouble. He could have fallen out of his chair with drowsiness, spent 15 minutes daydreaming, or read a whole page before he recognized it was meaningless.

Once the warning bell was sounded, the good learner has a whole array of specific actions he can take — more active processing, shifting tasks, relaxation procedures or using a variety of organizational or mnemonic skills. The poor learner has only a few alternatives — quitting, going to bed or indulging in whatever distracted him in the first place. So let's recap the differences between the two:

1. Good learners have self-monitoring programs that blow the whistle more quickly than poor learners.
2. They have programs that offer more options compared to poor learners.

Fenker's Fabulous Formula for Outfoxing Failure!

Here's how to establish a good self-monitoring program in three simple steps:

1. **Set your goal.** This should be a fairly immediate short-term goal such as reading a book (or a chapter), writing a short paper, solving a set of math problems or learning your French vocabulary for one lesson. Avoid vague, long-term goals such as "understanding" calculus, "doing better" in biology or being a "success" in college.

2. **Monitor the learning processes necessary to reach the goal.** Learn to recognize what's hindering you. When you begin to detour, be aware of it. I call this the GOTCHA point. A good monitoring program should immediately note the distraction and yell, GOTCHA! You're getting sidetracked again. Get back on the glory road." And it must keep yelling until it has your attention.

3. **Make a decision as to what you'll do.** When your monitor does

blow the whistle, (a) return to the original task, (b) select another task more fitted to your state of mind, (c) return to the original task but with a new processing strategy, or (d) stop and rest.

If your attention wanders momentarily, it may be enough to just note the fact and return to work. That first *GOTCHA* may be sufficient. But most likely, it's a cue that your learning method isn't active enough. Perhaps you should be underlining or paraphrasing. Perhaps you could study another subject more effectively.

The answer is to apply the right self-monitoring program to each particular learning problem. Over my years of teaching, I've put together a group of such problems with a description of how my good learners have dealt with them. I've listed the problem, its symptoms, how to detect them and a corrective self-monitoring program. Take one for yourself. They're free!

1. **Problem:** The Great Procrastinator. Or how to get a marvelously slow start on any learning task.

Symptoms: Daydreaming at your desk, spending a great amount of time organizing materials, changing one learning place for another, getting a Coke before you start, making phone calls, cleaning your desk, waiting for that one perfect moment, waiting for the noise of your roommate banging his head against the wall to subside.

Gotcha point: Once you've decided to study, put a red flag on every action before you begin. They may be distractors. Look them over, evaluate them and, if they're not necessary, eliminate them. If symptoms persist, then give yourself a small amount of time in which you can "mess around" before you start. But when this time is up, begin working immediately.

Self-monitoring program: "It's time to start studying but I'd better call Bill, otherwise he may call me when I'm working. *GOTCHA!* That's an excuse. I'll call him after I'm through. Hmmm . . . it might be better to study in the library, this room is messy and noisy. *GOTCHA!* That's another excuse. I was in the library 30 minutes ago and decided it was too quiet. I'll study here and not be disturbed by the mess or noise."

Comments: Procrastination often results when we are faced with what we consider a difficult task. You have put off studying philosophy because you know you'll have to concentrate very hard on the material. Here's how to beat that problem: Make molehills out of mountains. Say to yourself, "I won't even try to understand it. I'll simply go through and underline the key points at a quick pace. Then, I'll go back and examine these points and try to paraphrase them. I won't waste a lot of time trying to comprehend difficult new material. I'll leave the tough stuff for later." Aim at a relatively easy task instead of a difficult one. You'll recognize that after these preliminaries, the tough stuff has suddenly become much easier. And further, each successive pass through the material now permits you to attain a deeper understanding.

2. **Problem:** Famous Distractors I have known. Or, I'd rather slit my wrist (very lightly) than finish this assignment.

Symptoms: Sleepiness, generalized procrastination, need for social contact, abnormal hunger and thirst, remembering the once-in-a-lifetime opportunity to see the third rerun of the "Gong Show" that has the tap-dancing mortician.

Gotcha point: Beware of any feeling or activity that directs your attention from your study, regardless of its apparent importance. Be suspicious of any activity requiring your immediate attention. Unless it's a matter of life or death, recognize that you have been momentarily distracted and get back to work.

Self-monitoring program: "I've worked on this calculus problem for 15 minutes. What a waste. Only two more days until the 12th annual, formal buffalo stampede. Man, that'll be fun. *GOTCHA!* My mind is wandering. Get back on track. Daydreaming can wait. This philosophy is interesting but it's sure tough to understand. I don't have class tomorrow, so I really don't need to study now. I'll work much better tomorrow night, and HEY, that great beach party movie is on TV, "Surf's Up" with the Lemming family, Ari, Barry, Harry, Carrie, Gary, Kerrie, Larry, Mary, Perry, Terry . . . *GOTCHA!* Those are just excuses to keep from working. I decided earlier that it would take at least two nights to understand this stuff. I'll try to improve my concentration by asking questions as I go along to check my understanding."

Comments: Remember, no one is more clever than you at thinking up apparently valid reasons why you should put off a task or direct your attention elsewhere. Recognize this cleverness, and let your self-monitoring program be one step ahead.

3. **Problem:** I've read this page a dozen times already, and only a genius could understand this stuff.

Symptoms: Rereading a passage several times, seeking out attractive distractors, looking for pictures or diagrams to help explain the text, considering dropping the course.

Gotcha point: Beware of a trend toward flight when you finish a page after hard concentration that produces little understanding. Note the desire to throw up your hands. Listen for your inner voice to scream, "What the heck does that mean?"

Self-monitoring program: "That last page simply didn't make any sense. It seems to be conceptual rather than descriptive. Maybe instead of wasting my time, I should see Arbuckle tomorrow morning before class. He's a brain and can probably explain it to me in about 30 seconds. *GOTCHA* Okay, maybe I should read this page more slowly and include some form of active processing (underlining, outlining, paraphrasing, asking questions) to force my brain to assimilate this new information instead of just skimming the surface."

These are only a few examples of common problems. Later on we'll get down to some specific learning strategies that can be used effectively with these self-monitoring programs.

You didn't even touch on such problems as "My room's on fire (or if it isn't, I'll make sure it is)" or "I feel I'm coming down with terminal acne" or "I believe termites have caused structural damage to my Eberhart Faber."[1]

---

[1]A deadly ending. Turn the page.

Chapter 6

Concentration

"Would you mind repeating" or "What's that you say?"

Now, we're going to start putting it all together, these methods for battling the forces which keep us from zeroing in on our goals. Let's consult Nurf for a minute. Nurf! Nurf?

Sorry. I was deep in conversation with myself. I find me utterly fascinating.

Okay, we're going to work on concentration. And I warn you, there will be a test at the end of the chapter. You will be required to read and understand a page from Einstein and Leopold's book on relativity while your right shoe is on fire, a Playboy Bunny is at your feet searching for her costume and you're standing in the center of the Lawrence Welk band as it plays "Stars and Stripes Forever."[1]

We've been discussing how to reduce the influence of external and internal distractors and how self-monitoring can be used to minimize their effects. Now, we're going to get into the ways we can develop good concentration habits. Okay, what do you think concentration is?

Well, for openers, I'd say concentration is the ability to focus your attention on whatever you're doing.

That's pretty good, but it is missing one key ingredient — the "how-to-do-it." Let's go a little further with our definition. Concentration is the skill of effectively applying self-monitoring techniques to learning tasks. [2]

It's the use of these techniques to eliminate distractors, to cope with our bad habits and to do things that are appropriate for our level of attention and involvement.

Nurf's definition left out the "process" that permits you to focus your attention on a particular task. You can't will yourself to concentrate and automatically expect everything except the job at hand to disappear from your consciousness.

The learning process requires continual monitoring of distractors and activity

---

[1]This is a standard Fenker test and is usually given without the band showing up. In this case, Nurf needs all the help he can get.

[2]Please note that Dr. Fenker's definition is quite narrow, justifiably so, since his book is about learning. This same statement, however, would apply equally well to other activities such as driving, sports, sex, etc.

levels. Good learners and poor learners face the same problems. But, the good learner will develop effective self-monitoring programs for keeping on track, or at least to avoid getting far off track. Poor learners will typically wander all over the field.

Before I describe how concentration strategies work, let's examine several "classic techniques." These are useful guides that fit just about everyone.

(1) **The old work place.** This means picking out a special place as a work area — a desk, the library, a study carrel, even the john. When you're there, you will do only study or work related projects. No writing letters, no daydreaming, no listening to records. If you have to do these things, then go somewhere else to do them. You'll find after a while, this work place will come to serve as a stimulus for effective concentration.

Feckless[1] Fenker's Fantastic Fables — I recommended this approach to a sorority pledge class that had a poor scholastic record. The entire group decided to try it and chose the library rather than the sorority house as their work place. But occasionally other students would wander in and sit at one of these special tables.

The sorority girls handled the problem by talking and making such a commotion that the intruders would usually leave. Then, the fraternities figured out what was going on and sent groups of "table breakers" to disrupt studying. The result was a low key war-of-the-sexes with little studying and much flirtation.

That was about the sorriest example I ever heard of to disprove a point. May I suggest your advice isn't worth the recycled paper it's written on?

To the contrary! Despite all the hassles, the project was a success. The sorority jumped from last to third place in academic standing during the semester.[2]

(2) **One time, one task.** You establish a regular time for studying and always use that time for learning rather than for other tasks. When it comes to "X" o'clock, it's time to go to your work place and open the books. The study periods don't have to be long, but they should be in blocks of time you can control — time that is as free from interruption as possible. For example, the only free time I found to write this book

---

[1]Feckless. One who has had his feck surgically removed.

[2]C'et a rire. Suckered you right in, didn't he, Nurf? Dr. Fenker failed to mention, however, that the library was a wreck afterwards and decided to ban all future study groups.

was very early in the morning be-tween 11:45 a.m. and 12:00 noon.

3. **Cut off the audio/visual noise.** Eliminate all distractors at the work place. This means everything that's likely to attract your attention and reduce concentration. Pictures, let-ters, magazines, radio, phonograph, a window, or your roommate's voice, particularly if it sounds like Phyllis Diller.

These are basic useful techniques, but relying on this type of external control to

improve concentration is like putting a Ferrari body on a Model-T frame and en-gine. The streamlining may help, but the fundamental problems that produced poor concentration habits will remain.

Now, let's get back to the definition of concentration that included the process that permits one to focus attention on a particular task.

Concentration and activity levels.

Just how much concentration a task will require usually is determined by the activ-ity level of that task. Flying a plane, driv-ing in a race or juggling three sticks of dynamite calls for considerable concentra-tion. And the penalty for relaxing your concentration can be most unpleasant.

So we can say, in general, you're less likely to let your mind wander in a high activity task than you are in a more pas-sive task such as watching TV or reading a book. If you fall asleep while reading, the consequences are minimal compared to what would happen if you dozed during the car race.

An important technique for improving concentration, then, is to force yourself to increase your level of involvement. You can do this by either shifting to a more ac-tive task, or by changing an inherently passive task into a more active form.

For example, instead of just reading, in-crease your activity level by underlining. This is one of the most crucial self-mon-itoring skills to learn — finding an activity level which matches your concentration abilities for each learning task.

You use lousy examples. Just try underlining comic books; that cheap paper tears every time.

I'm surprised, Nurf, I didn't know blunt Crayolas were that destructive.

Now, from what we have said, you can see that it is not necessary to eliminate all distractors in order to concentrate. Instead, concentration depends on how effectively you can deal with distractors once they occur. Certainly, reducing their numbers and frequency can help. But you're the one who has to learn how to handle them.

Imagine this scene. We place a young lady who is good at concentration in a noisy room and assign a book to read. Our volunteer gives the appearance of reading without any distraction. Yet, if we stopped the background conversation at any point, and asked our reader what subject is being discussed, surprisingly, she will probably know the topic and have some information about the last few sentences spoken.

Our reader was attending primarily to the book but was aware of many other things, including the background conversations. Her effective self-monitoring programs prevented her attention from shifting to the conversation even though parts of it entered her consciousness. It's almost as if the words or sounds floated through her consciousness and never be-

came anchored until a word with a very high importance value came by — sex, her name, sex.

And then what happened? For fear of missing something good, her self-monitoring program will shift attention to the conversation. You've probably listened to lecturers who used spicy words and expressions, even violent gestures or noises, to capture your attention in case it had wandered.

Writers use this technique also. For example: *(EDITOR'S NOTE: THE AUTHOR'S EXAMPLE OF THIS TRICK AS APPLIED TO WRITING HAS BEEN DELETED BECAUSE OF VIOLATION OF STATE STATUTES.)*[1]

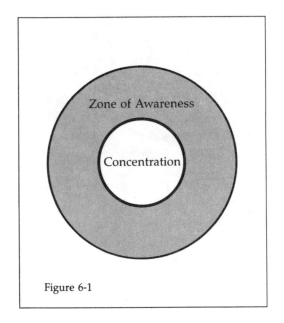

Figure 6-1

---

[1]See City of Trafney Falls vs. Max Edison and the phonograph.

I'm sure this example gives a complete explanation of my point. What we've been talking about can be described graphically. Take a look at Figure 6-1. Obviously, this drawing cannot be taken too literally, for we've found no evidence yet that inside your head is a neat set of concentric circles properly labeled . . . or improperly labeled, for that matter. We have found a few hollow heads, however. Nurf's, for example.

It was only a frontal lobotomy, Fenker.

The center circle or "Zone of Concentration" represents that part of your consciousness that's focused on the learning task. The outer circle, "Zone of Awareness," represents those things you are aware of but are not concentrating on. Many sounds, sights, smells, and so on, enter this zone of awareness, but they don't receive your full attention.

The smaller, shaded circle represents a buffer zone provided by self-monitoring programs. They control the flow of internal and external stimulation competing for your attention. These programs act like shields and reflect potential distractors before they can have any impact.

Fenker, my congratulations! You have just reinvented the TV commercial for headache pain, pain, pain, which gets relief fast, fast, fast. All you need is a little hammer whanging away at the top.

Notice how I ignore this distractor and concentrate on the task of imparting wisdom. There's a fine line which distinguishes monitoring programs which are so automatic you are not consciously aware of them from programs that do require some attention on your part. For example, I know a man who consciously tuned out his wife's voice until the process became unconscious and automatic. He is essentially deaf to her, but to no one else. In fact, you can't believe how quiet it is around our house anymore.

Thus, you may be able to ignore background noises produced by wind, radio and cars without calling conscious attention to the task. Yet, ignoring your roommate's telephone conversation with her boyfriend may require a conscious effort on your part and a shift in activity level. Or it may even mean changing your location.

Finally and wisely, it may be impossible to ignore certain crucial signals such as your name, shouts of "fire" or the sound of a large and hairy animal panting in your ear.

I have a friend with a large and hairy animal that I will sic on your ear if you don't get around to the great concentration strategies you promised. Can't you focus on the task at hand?

One more thing, Nurf. This is too important to omit because it's the basic principle which underlies the development of

65

good concentration habits no matter what strategies you decide to use.

DON'T REWARD LEARNING BEHAVIORS WHICH REPRESENT POOR CONCENTRATION STRATEGIES. If you find yourself using a poor concentration method, don't reward its use by terminating it with some more pleasant activity.

Let me explain. Suppose you're studying a history assignment and discover that your level of concentration is so poor you are having to reread each page several times. You might then decide it's time for a break and head immediately for the refrigerator or the TV. What's happened? You're rewarding yourself for poor concentration, because this was the event that preceeded taking a break! This means that in the future you are more likely to adopt a poor concentration strategy!

Reward only good concentration

If you are serious about improving your study habits, reward only the use of good concentration strategies. For example, here's how an effective strategy might work. Imagine that you are reading a biology assignment and concentrating poorly. Your monitoring program notes the lapse in concentration and produces self-talk something like this, "I'm not getting it together. I've read this page four times. I need a rest. But, before I stop, I'm going to read at least two more pages with really

good concentration."

Obviously, there is a connection between poor concentration — reading a page four times — and taking a break. But the strongest linkage is between good concentration — reading the last two pages — and rewarding yourself with a break.

So the word is: reward only good habits. If a bad habit persists, weaken it by gradually associating it with some more desirable behavior. Remember that often the most important reward is to cease studying. Avoid situations where poor learning behavior brings this about. Always try to end your studying after a successful learning trip (even if it's only a short one), rather than as an excuse for an unfortunate detour.

Fenker's sackful of successful strategies

Here are the concentration strategies my students and I find give the best results. Examine the whole sackful. Then, pick those methods that fit your learning style and problems. Practice them at every opportunity and reward only your good attempts.

1. **Short But Sweet.** It's better to tackle a brief task on which you can concentrate fully than a longer one on which your concentration waxes and wanes.[1]

---

[1] Waxes and wanes are on aisle five just next door to soaps, detergents and cleansers. If you don't find what you're looking for, please call the manager.

Study for the amount of time you have designated as your attention span. If your attention is ready to wander at the end of this period, let it. Relax a few minutes. Then, go at it again. On the other hand, if you're still concentrating well at the end of this period, keep going a few more minutes. You'll find that with a little practice, you can gradually increase your concentration span for most subjects.

So your short and sweet goals for concentration are to practice good habits for short periods and then gradually develop this capacity for longer periods.

I tried this strategy and the results were disasterous! I started with one minute of concentration and a three minute break. The concentration period worked well, but I found it necessary to lengthen the break to 30 minutes. It took me three days to read the instructions for my math assignment.

Here's how to make it work:

Try to identify your "concentration span" for various learning tasks. This is the amount of time you're able to concentrate fully without having your attention wander. Obviously, it will vary from task to task. Mine varies from one minute for history to several hours for the current issue of *Penthouse*. Don't worry if you need to start with a very limited span for some of your difficult subjects. That's normal.

Okay, then, be warned: the short-but-sweet strategy requires a set of self-monitoring skills and some common sense. First, when you begin a period of concentration, your self-monitoring programs should insure that you start immediately. If you spend 10 minutes fiddling around for a three minute concentration period, the odds are you'll never get to see "Johnny Carson." Next, it should detect when you stop concentrating and then, order you to return immediately to the task. You must learn that a break in concentration is not to be used as an excuse for resting or daydreaming. It's simply another distractor that must be dealt with promptly and effectively.

2) **Eat Your Vegetables Before Dessert.** This is a similar approach in that the concentration span may be very brief. However, once your concentration has lapsed, you establish a finite goal — say, to read one more page. You then continue concentrating until this goal is reached, and only then, do you take a break. To improve your concentration, you can gradually lengthen the task that must be completed after the original lapse. Thus, you may eventually require yourself to read four pages or finish a chapter before you rest.

Your self-talk might go like this: "Sshhee! It's hard to concentrate tonight. Already my mind has wandered to washing my hair, trying that new shampoo concentrate with the Oil of Beaver Haunch Conditioner, to the new guy I saw in the toiletry section of the drugstore. Wonder if he works there every afternoon. Hold it! Vegetables before dessert!! I'm not going to think about him until I finish at least a good part of this assignment on 'Medieval Archways as Effective Dust Catchers.' I'll make

myself read three more pages before resting."

It'll produce results. Knowing you can break in just three pages will give you an incentive to finish them quickly. And this, in turn, may increase your attentiveness or concentration level.

The major advantage of this method over the Short But Sweet strategy is that your goal is a specific task to be accomplished — pages, problems, words — rather than simply time spent. With a little experience, you can increase the requirements so you can complete quite a large task after you notice your concentration is slipping. And you're rewarding both good concentration and good completion behavior — two of the most important skills in the arsenal of an effective learner.

3. **The DST/DST Method.** Don't Sit There, Do Something, Turkey! This is probably the easiest to use. Lapses in concentration often result when you are doing something that isn't sufficiently active or engaging. The activity of your hands, eyes and mind isn't enough to keep your attention focused on learning.

You've probably driven down a stretch of road which seems to go on and on in a straight line. If it doesn't bore you to death, it puts you to sleep. After a couple of headjerks[1] or surviving a wild sashay out into a field before getting back on the road, you're going to do something to keep yourself a little more alert. You turn on the radio, read signboards aloud or hum dirty songs.

You've shifted your activity level from simply driving to driving plus something else. The purpose is to keep your mind alert, active and at least partially focused on the road. The same principle applies to learning tasks. When a task becomes so boring that it doesn't engage your mind and your eyes take on a dazed appearance, then DON'T SIT THERE, DO SOMETHING, TURKEY! Shift to a more active form of learning. It will help keep your attention focused on the material.

Research makes it clear that an actively engaged mind learns much more effectively than a passive one. You will learn more and faster when you are not operating like a sponge. BEWARE THE GLASSY-EYED SYNDROME.

Let me point out the plight of the pitiful passive learner. He sets aside, say, ten minutes to study his favorite subject. He opens the text, flips slowly through the pages with an intent, but glassy look in his eye and prays his mind will absorb something. The time passes and nothing happens.

Sounds ridiculous? Almost one-third of my students report the majority of their study time is spent in this state! It's a tragedy because invariably, these students are making poor grades. Thus, they have to spend an enormous amount of time studying — to make up for these poor habits.

Often these glassy-eyed students can spend hours in this dazed state without even recognizing a yawn as a sleep cue telling them it's time to switch strategies. A good learner would detect the passive state quickly and shift to a more active procedure. Remember, passive learners have to spend much more time studying than do more active learners.

"Active" actions

Here are some things you can do to increase your level of activity. Practice them! Remember, if you are not using an active learning strategy, you are wasting your time studying. Either learn actively or do something else. But DST/DST!

- Underline or highlight.
- Mark or write in the margins.
- Organize the contents.
- Outline chapters.
- Paraphrase orally or in writing.
- Form imagery associations.
- Construct mnemonics.

---

[1]Principals, Full Professors, Department Heads, and Deans may be included in this category.

- Form questions and get answers.
- Imagine yourself teaching the material to someone.
- Diagram relationships between parts of the text.
- Apply a comprehension language.

Have you noticed this book contains many devices to help keep you awake as a reader? Headings, subheads, Nurf, Gorbish, numbers, etc.

Thanks a lot, Fenker, it's the first time I've been equated with an "etc."[1]

4. **The Grass is Greener.** Your lapses in concentration may be the result of boredom, fatigue or saturation with the subject you're studying. The GIG technique requires switching to a new and perhaps more stimulating task. It's similar to the DST/DST method except that you shift subjects, rather than activity level. It's an appropriate title because it's easy to abuse its usefulness by continually wishing to be doing something else. Shifting every five minutes can help your attention, but it also can be extremely disruptive. Break up your study assignments into a series of short (20 minute to 30 minute) periods. This strategy can be effective, but don't overdo it.

5. **Lights out.** We touched on this back in Chapter 3, in discussing internal distractors. Problem: You have a dozen ideas on your mind, you're highly anxious or you have a major emotional crisis. Bring your attention back to the learning task through self-talk and relaxation. Here's the procedure:

a. Find a comfortable place and go through the relaxation exercises described in Chapter 2. When you're completely relaxed, give yourself the following instructions. Tell yourself:

- To temporarily remove all problems, anxieties and distracting feelings from your mind.
- That you will handle these at another more appropriate time.
- That it's irrational to attempt to resolve everything at once and that your first and most immediate problem is to complete your study assignments.
- That once you're finished studying, you can attempt to deal with these other problems (if they still need attention) and
- That you will find it much easier to concentrate when you wake up.

b. Wake up.

c. Continue working.

---

[1]This is a typographical error. Nurf has often been equated with an "ecch!"

There are many ways to skin a cat, including both the classic methods and the procedures we've covered in this section. But there is one crucial self-talk program all these methods have in common. This is the program that separates the good concentrators from the poor. Although we've mentioned it previously, it's so important that I've outlined its major steps.

- You're concentrating on a task.
- For some reason your concentration lapses.
- Your self-monitoring system quickly notices and directs your attention back to the task.
- You return to concentrating on the task.

The key is the word "quickly." Good learners pick up the lapses more quickly than poor learners. And they are armed with a variety of strategies for beginning concentration again.

Right, Nurf? Nurf??

What?

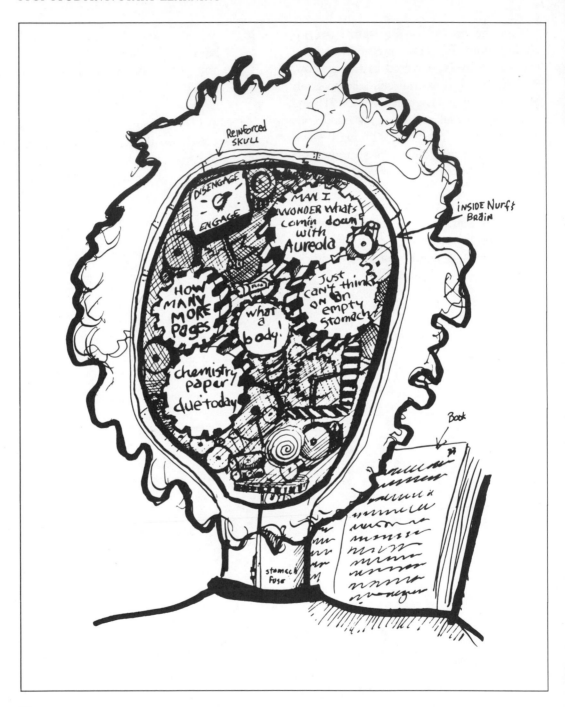

Chapter 7

Memory

"Let me see now . . . "

Fenker, I'm in deep trouble. I clean forgot Aureola's birthday Friday. And she's ready to kill me. I knew it was sometime along about now, but I just forgot the date.

You mean you couldn't remember?

No, I just forgot it.

You couldn't remember.

Look, Fenker, I forgot it. I remember everything else about that woman — what she likes to eat, drink, her favorite books, her measurements.

Measurements?

37-35-25-36

That's odd. Do you mean 37-35-36?

No, with her you read across and down. She also sort of walks on the bias.

Memory is a strange phenomenon. We're not certain how it works, although we have some idea of the mechanics. It is responsible for the creation of new words in our vocabulary, such as "Whatshisname," "whatchamacallit," "thingamajig" or "doohickey," which are used to try to induce another person in a conversation to use her memory to assist in finding the word or phrase you can't remember.

Memory is our own personal rerun of the past. It is the stuff reminiscences are made of. It can be as elusive as quicksilver. And, far too often, it just doesn't work when we want it to. It's true, as in Nurf's case that we usually remember what we consider to be important or interesting or the details of events which have had a strong emotional impact on us. But unless we make a specific effort to nail down facts, figures, names, etc., we tend not to remember most of the details of the tens of thousands of sensory impressions we receive every day.

You might believe that by now your need for good memory skills in school is diminishing. No way. The sad truth is that 75 to 90 percent of your work in high school and college involves memorization of material. Yes, even at this advanced stage of your education, where most subjects are of a conceptual nature, you're still going to have to develop muscles on your memory. Why? Because instructors often equate "understanding" with memorization, especially where concepts are concerned.

So, what is memory? It is the process we use to "store" or "save" or "retain" knowledge or information. Normally, we think of memory processes as having two distinct stages. First, there is the coding or storage of information as described above. Second, there is the recall of this information at a later time, and here is the mighty "rub." Many of my students believe their memory skills are poor because they "forget" information that was once learned. To this, I reply "Humbug!"[1] The information hasn't simply disappeared as the word "forgot" suggests. It's probably still stored in your brain. The real problem is that you cannot recall it or bring it forth when needed.

It's in there somewhere

It is difficult to measure just how much information is in your memory, but many researchers believe it contains virtually everything you have previously learned or experienced. There's plenty of room. Our brain contains something like ten billion neurons (and therefore, almost an infinite number of combinations of circuits).

A researcher named Penfield came up with some fascinating results while operating on patients to remove damaged portions of their brains. He discovered that a very small electrical stimulus applied to certain areas of the cortex would often cause the patient to report in great detail an event experienced some years earlier.

By changing the location of the electrical probe, a variety of different memories could be evoked. Surprisingly, the majority of these memory experiences elicited information the patients thought had been lost. These memories included such things as a detailed record of a phone conversation, a grocery list, music or a meal experienced many years earlier and assumed to be long forgotten! And, we read almost daily of police psychologists placing a witness to a crime under hypnosis to secure detailed descriptions of the scene, the principals and the sequence of events.

The problem we face is this: while we do not often "forget" materials once learned, this information is often stored so as to be difficult or impossible to recall. Thus, developing a good memory depends on learning material in such a way that it can be retrieved. High emotional levels make it easy to recall what we were doing the day Dallas played host to President Kennedy, but what about other less poignant dates, such as Washington's birthday seven years ago? Or, try to dredge up the date of the Battle of Hastings, the value of pi to five decimal places, the 36th element on the atomic periodic

---

[1] Fenker is given to such expletives. It's not known if this is because of a paucity of vocabulary or if his mother was traumatized by a poor road company version of *A Christmas Carol*.

table or the name of Tom Swift's handyman.[1] Tough, isn't it?

Kinds of memory

Let's see if I can remember what I learned in college about the kinds of memory we are blessed or cursed with. Scientists believe there are three types — iconic, short term and long term.

Iconic. This is a form of photographic memory of very short duration — probably less than a second. If I presented a picture on the screen for a few seconds and then immediately after removing it, pointed an arrow at the place where a particular object was located, you could correctly identify that object with considerable accuracy. If I waited even one second to flash the arrow, however, you would probably not recall the object.

Short Term. This is the immediate memory for visual and auditory information and lasts only a few seconds. It apparently is limited to about seven items. If a friend says, "My phone number is 555-9346," and then in a few seconds asks you to repeat the number, the chances are you will recall it correctly. If he waits 30 seconds or a minute to ask, you probably

would be unable to recall the number.[2]

Try this: Read the first telephone number below then look away for five seconds and try to repeat it. You probably will have little difficulty. Next, read the second number; but this time turn away for a minute. Most people will not be able to recall the number correctly. Now, look at the third number and turn away for a minute, while repeating the number to yourself mentally several times. You'll probably be right because this is one of the techniques for converting information from short term to long term memory.

246-3766
837-9268
316-4815

Long term. This is the most important kind of memory for learning. Information stored in long term memory is thought to be permanently available to us. However, it's not unusual for items we assumed to be "memorized" to be unavailable to us at critical times, such as on an examination. Why? One reason is that we often confuse what we call "rote" and "meaningful" memory tasks. And as Nurf discovered, information which is entered into long-term memory in a "rote" fashion may not be accessible or usable when you need it — even though it is still stored.

---

[1]Eradicate Sampson. So there!

[2]I don't want to be pushy, Dr. Fenker, but I have a memory technique for numbers. I have found it effective to break them up into groups of two — i.e., 36-25-34 or 38-25-34.

Rote vs meaningful learning

Probably the most important classification of memory-related tasks is into the following two groups: meaningful tasks and rote tasks. You undoubtedly know what rote memorization requires. Given a horrendous list of dates, terms, foreign vocabulary or parts of the anatomy of the cross-eyed, sugarless beetle to remember, you may find that the list is completely novel; that is, it does not seem related to, anything you have learned previously (or care much about learning presently). You are forced, therefore, to memorize the list verbatim in a "rote" manner without the aid of prior background knowledge or a conceptual framework for relating the terms or vocabulary.

Often, when you study a subject for the first time, you must adopt a rote strategy since the vocabulary and concepts are unfamiliar. As you acquire some background knowledge and familiarity with the terms, your later learning will be easier because new concepts and terms will "fit" with the background knowledge. Memorization that is related to or in some way fits with previously learned material is called "meaningful."

So let's put it in the form of a rule: Meaningful learning occurs when you have a structure or framework for organizing the new material because of your previous experience with similar or related materials. For example a friend points out his car and says "Remember it so you can locate it later in the parking lot." You would have little difficulty. You might note the color, make, model year and perhaps the license. Based on your previous experience, you know that these particular attributes are the most useful in identifying a specific car. This memory process is meaningful because your previous knowledge of cars provides a way to classify new instances so you can readily identify them later.

Remembering just one car is no job. Why there's a guy in Washington who recalled more than three million cars last year.

Cool it, Nurf. Suppose, however, you had never seen an automobile before. You might decide, unwisely, to remember your friend's car on the basis of such features as the number of tires, the color of the bumper, or the shape of the steering wheel. Obviously, these would be of little help in discriminating autos. So, it's the framework for interpreting and organizing new material that makes your memory task easier.

Make it easy.

It's relatively simple to learn and remember the materials which relate or connect in a meaningful way to your present knowledge. Therefore I'm going to give you the tools to help identify the connections between old and new materials . . . AND develop new connections where none exist.

Before we start, however, I want you to

recognize that most books are written in a way that makes them very helpful. They encourage you to form connections through the principle of organization. You're provided with a chapter summary, a list of key ideas or an outline which you can skim before reading a chapter. Each of these devices gives you a kind of framework to help you interpret and organize the material. You may have done the same thing yourself — constructing your own frameworks and organizational schemes. These methods work because each item to be remembered can later be found either (1) because of its unique characteristics or (2) because of its connection with the organizational scheme. It's sort of a mental Easter egg hunt — you search your memory until the appropriate material turns up.

Associations: memory glue

There is an important principle in describing how memory works — association. In fact, some authors contend that all memory is based on association. What is it? Association refers to the connections or links between terms, concepts or images you have stored in your memory.

Here are a few examples. Associations of:
SIMILARITY — chicken, duck, goose, turkey.
SEMANTIC MEANING — chicken; wings, feathers, beak, claws.
BIOLOGICAL CLASSIFICATION — flowers; rose, tulip, orchid
YOUR EXPERIENCE — baseball: summer, crowds, hotdogs, scoring.

Associations are much easier to form when there is a meaningful, "common sense" connection between items. Because of this, abstract or intangible items are often difficult to remember. Also, let's say it again: rote learning tasks are difficult and time consuming because there is no structural framework for interpreting new material. A list of groceries, biology terms or people at a party is difficult to remember because it's hard to establish meaningful associations between these items and what's already in your mind.

What's the solution when you need to memorize rote or abstract material?

Fenker's Fantastic Framework for Making Rote Really Right

One solution (used by professional memory experts) is this: Create a special framework or structure in your mind that can be used for all rote tasks. This framework can then be linked to new material. The learning process then is no longer rote, because you are forming a set of meaningful associations! And more — these special frameworks can be used over and over for many types of material just by creating an appropriate set of associations.

Fenker, you have the ability to cloud men's minds. Would you mind setting these "special frameworks" out in the bright light of day so we unannointed can profit from your brilliance?

My pleasure. Let's take a few:

Mnemonics.   This is the simplest case. Mnemonics involves the use off a key word or phrase to represent a set of words or items to be remembered. And it works! The letters in the word or the first letters of the words in a phrase correspond to the first letters in the word or the first letters of the items to be remembered. For example, name the Great Lakes. You can't. Then, remember the word *HOMES*. Now it's easy. *Huron, Ontario, Michigan, Erie, Superior.*

Pilots use the word *GUMP* in their landing checklist: Gas, Undercarriage, Mixture, Prop. It's simple and extremely effective for short lists. In these cases, the order isn't important. But on the other hand, suppose you were in an astronomy class and you were charged with remembering the order of the stages of the typical star's life cycle. Someone (bless his name) developed a mnemonic for that: *"Oh, Be A Fine Girl and Give Me a Kiss."* The stages are *O, B, A, F, G, M, K.*

You're a dirty old star gazer . . . a celestial Peeping Tom.

I spent a long time peering through a telescope in my younger days, and I will testify that the focal length of the lens can range from millions of light years to only 100 feet across the street to the third floor of the girls' dorm.

With a little practice, you can create mnemonics for any set of terms and concepts you might choose to remember. The mnemonics represent the "framework" we're talking about, a word or simple phrase that is easy to remember because of its familiarity. The letters or words in the mnemonics are each associated with other less common words you want to remember.

What are the four voices in a quartet? STAB: Soprano, Tenor, Alto, Bass. Clever. Okay, how about a grocery list: soup, towels, eggs, roast beef, nuts and orange juice.

STERNO! And, that's probably what they'd taste like if you mix them together.

I don't want to mislead you. Constructing mnemonics is not all that easy because of two problems which limit their usefulness. First, the job of making one up can be quite time-consuming, because each new set of items requires a different mnemonic. When the list of items exceeds five or six words, it may be very difficult to find the appropriate mnemonic word or phase.

Second, it may not be a very informative association. Even if each letter in the mnemonic represents the first letter in the word or phrase, you may need to know more than just the first letter to recall the word or phrase. Do you want to go through life saying, "I can't remember the word, but it begins with "G!" Thus, if we consider an association to be a link between something new you want to remember and something already in your memory, mnemonics can often be very weak links.

Linking. A link is the association between something you want to remember and something already in your memory. As we mentioned above, if the best you can do is to remember it's a word that starts with a "G,"' then the link is very weak. One way to create stronger "chains" is by forming a collection of imaginary associations known as a "linking system."

For example, here's an illustration from an excellent book[1] on memory by Harry Loring and Jerry Lucas. Consider the following list of words — airplane, tree, envelope, earring, bucket, sing, basketball, salami, star and nose. Notice that the words in this list have no association or connection that implies a sequence. Therefore, to use this system we must learn to link words in correct order.

Here's how to do it: We use our imagination to picture an association between the first and second words. For example, you might form a mental picture of an AIRPLANE crashing into a TREE. Next, to associate a TREE to an ENVELOPE, you might imagine opening an envelope and finding the tree or imagine the leaves on a tree being shaped like envelopes. Go through the list in this way,

---

[1] It is, indeed, a fine book, although right now I can't recall its name. But, it probably will come to me. If and when it does, I'll jump right in and let you know. I think it starts with a "B."

linking each item with the previous and following items on the list. Try it on this ten-word list and see how quickly you can learn it.

Once you have mastered the basic system, you have a powerful memory framework available for your use. Because the framework is arbitrary, it can be used with an unlimited variety of items or concepts you wish to remember.

So, let's review the procedure:
1. Form an association between each of the items you want to remember and a corresponding word in the linking system.
2. If the order is important, be sure the linking system order matches the correct item order.

Now, surprise! After forming these associations, you have effectively memorized the list. How can you recall each item? By simply going through the sequence of links in the order you learned. And once you've learned the system and developed some skill at forming associations, you'll be amazed how quickly you can learn words dates and concepts.

You have transformed rote learning into a psuedo-meaningful task. At the outset you had no framework for interpreting or organizing information. And by definition, you should have found it impossible to establish associations between the old and new material. But you developed a "phony" framework. And this did the job. The associations you formed may be arbitrary and bizarre and in no way related to the meaning of the new material. Yet, they can make it easy to recall the new items. Linking systems are great for learning names, lists of technical terms, numbers, dates and foreign vocabularies.

The Marvelous Magician of the Mind

You've probably seen one of those incredible memory experts perform. I met one at a banquet in Chicago. Before dinner he visited each table and introduced himself to each guest. After dinner, as part of the evening's entertainment, he quickly ticked off the names and hometowns of each person at the banquet. This was quite some feat. There were over 100 guests! He did it by association. Later, when the show finished, I asked him how he had remembered one name that seemed especially difficult. The man, Homer Fitzgerald of Oshkosk, Wisconsin, was fat and beerfaced. Our expert laughed and said "That was easy. I pictured a man opening up a bottle of 'Home(r)' brew which 'Fitz(ed)' up his nose causing him to sneeze, 'Oshkosh.'" He was definitely ready for admission to the home for the over-weird. But that same technique can get you an "A" and be a rather fun way to do things as well.

Meaningful learning tasks.

Just as I had a mild disclaimer about mnemonics, let me do the same with linking systems. You may not need them as much as you think because a majority of your learning will involve material with which you already have some experience. Or you will find that developing a framework will be an inherent part of the learning task.

This is obviously true for college learning where you may have already had anywhere from eight to twelve years of prior experience in such subjects as math, English, history and science.

Many meaningful learning methods are also based on association. You have the framework, so your problem now is how best to link or associate new information. In this case, the emphasis should be on techniques which help create new associations rapidly and methods for making them strong and permanent.

These techniques are referred to as methods for "elaboration." And they're easy to understand and simple to use. Let's have a go at them.

1. **Imagery.** This is the most important of the elaboration techniques. Imagery is the process of trying to form pictures in your mind of objects, words or scenes. It's the attempt to use your mind, instead of your eyes, to visualize things. Close your eyes. Picture an elephant named Nurfo, with blue polka dots.

Careful, Fenker.

No problem. For some, the elephant will be clear and real looking and much like you'd see in a dream. For others, the

elephant may be very abstract, vague and hardly visible. But it makes no difference. Nurfo and the polka dots are still there. And he can be used in associations. It's a shame that we often lose this ability as we grow up. Children are usually able to form clearer visual images than adults. And it's probably because as they learn to read and write and think verbally, they cease to exercise their imagery skills.

Now, how does imagery improve the quality or durability of associations and help to form new ones rapidly? Let's say that for some strange reason, you want to associate an elephant and a golf ball. Try to picture in your mind a scene containing both. You might see the elephant trying to hit the golf ball with his trunk. Or you can imagine an elephant attempting to balance on a very, very, very large golf ball. If, in the future you are given one of these items (say a golf ball) and asked to re-

81

member the other item, you can simply form a mental picture of the scene in which the golf ball appeared. Guess what? There's a funny large animal with a trunk also in the picture. And, you know your correct response is "elephant."

You may have to be fairly creative to deal with more abstract items, but the principle is the same. Assume you want to associate the date 1849 with the California Gold Rush. You might visualize a group of prospectors in covered wagons filled with gold. Each prospector wears a t-shirt with the number 18 on the front. The 49 wagons are arranged in a seven-by-seven square. And you can imagine this wild-looking troup moving across the desert. It may sound complex, but such pictures

take only seconds to create. And once formed, they are nearly impossible to forget.

2. **Out of Proportion.** When you are visualizing items, make them very large or very small. Stretch them far out of proportion in order to make the images more unusual. In order to link an airplane with a tree, you might want to imagine a tree with airplanes for leaves or an airplane with leaves for wings.

3. **Exaggeration.** Make your images as unusual or bizarre as possible. If your item has a particularly prominent feature, exaggerate it to help you remember the links. Instead of one item, you might imagine a hundred, a thousand or millions. To link bucket and salami, visualize a large bucket filled with hundreds of sticks of salami.

4. **Action.** Make your images move, crash together or contact you in some way. Adding action helps bond the links created and makes the images easy to re-

member. Imagine an airplane crashing into a tree. To associate an elephant and golf ball, visualize an elephant shooting golf balls out of its trunk at you like a machine gun.

5. **Substitution.** Give the properties of one item in the link to the other item. To associate earring with basketball you might imagine a person wearing basketballs for earrings or imagine a basketball game where an earring was used as a hoop.

Elaboration techniques help strengthen the associations between items by giving the associations distinctive features. These features help anchor images in your memory. You may need to use several elaboration methods for one link in order to nail it down in your memory. If you've tried to visualize these examples without success, don't worry. Your imagination may just be rusty. Go through them again creating your own links. Practice helps.

I was framed.

Another technique to sharpen the edge of your memory in meaningful learning tasks is to understand how knowledge is organized before trying to memorize it. In other words, build the best association framework possible before you attempt to link new information to the structure.

As I mentioned earlier, many texts are written to provide you with a framework. Summaries of major points are often given in the beginning or ending of a chapter. Headings are set in bold-face print to guide you through the sequence of information. Organizational charts, diagrams and flow charts can all help you in organizing the material for easier retention. Interesting examples, drawings, and writing techniques relating your experiences all serve to help you form better associations and give you a head-start.

If you skim a chapter seeking out organizational cues before trying to read it in detail, you are building a framework that will help you in interpreting and remembering the material.

How much time should you spend in such skimming? Normally, at most, a few minutes. If you're having real trouble with a subject, it's probably worthwhile to try to outline the chapter before you start. When you then read it, you can change the outline where necessary and add details.

It's like studying a map before you take a trip. The map indicates the best route and points out the major landmarks you can expect to see. By knowing what you can expect to find on your route, you can determine if you're off the track. If you've skimmed a chapter for the highlights or organizational cues, it will be obvious when you miss those highlights in a later reading. (You'll also need to keep your self monitoring programs working.)

Digging it out.

Now that we've covered some methods of storing information, let's find out how to retrieve it when we want it. And let's go back to my argument with Nurf, who insisted he "forgot" Aureola's birthday.

I did forget. I just plain forgot.

You're just like all the rest, Nurf. You think your memory skills are poor because you forgot information you once learned. My response: Pfaugh! That's a crock. You haven't forgotten. It's still there in your long term memory. Your problem is that you can't recall it when it is needed.

Fenker says "Pfaugh"!

There are a number of books on learning which offer "retrieval" strategies for recalling information stored in long term memory. Frankly, I think that's like trying to close a gaping wound with a bandaid. If the information you want to recall wasn't learned in a proper manner — using organizational cues or an association framework — then, most of it is probably inaccessible. A retrieval strategy may help you recall a few tidbits of information, but not the entire set. So spend your time developing efficient learning techniques, and recall can be automatic.

Let me drag out our travel analogy again, even though it's getting pretty dog-eared. Imagine you're traveling through a very dense, large forest filled with interesting places to stop — hamburger stands, pizza shacks and parking lots. Once you've completed your tour of the forest, you might want to remember each place you visited so you can figure out where you got ptomaine poisoning. Or you might want to return to a particular location to recover the upper right incisor that fell out when you hit the bone in the deluxe Magnaburger. It would help in remembering these places if you developed some associations like people met, snacks eaten and activities enjoyed to make each place more distinctive.

It would also help if you had marked

your route and stops on a map. Then, you could simply trace back along your route as a guide for deciding what you did and when. That map now becomes a powerful organizational tool for boosting your ability to recall. Thus, in ordinary learning tasks, organizational frameworks or linking systems function much like a trip map. They provide a path through your memory with a number of stops or key points to which you can relate the details of your trip.

Fenker's Favorite Framework

Consider the following paragraph:
"Things that go bump in the night are usually frightening, but not always. Big noises such as windows breaking, doors slamming, furniture moving or heavy footsteps are scary. Small sounds can be scary when they appear unnatural or are made by unfamiliar persons or animals (or any more bizarre beings). Such noises include grunts, growls, high pitched whines, electronic sounds and strange heavy breathing. Friendly, small sounds include pets' noises, the faucet dripping, your clock ticking or ripe money falling off the tree in your living room."

Now, let's assume you want to remember all of those sounds. Here's how you do it:
Your first problem will be to remember

the framework. But usually this will be easy because you constructed it, and its parts will be logically related in some manner. You can use its categories to form specific associations with the sounds. Instead of trying to remember the total list of 15 "things that go bump in the night," you simply follow a path through the framework, stopping at each category where you have stored specific associations. Thus, as you reach "big, scary noises" or "small, friendly noises," you will pause to recall the sounds in each category.

What's really going on?

Let's dig a little deeper into how organization and association are related. Associations form what I call the "glue" or substance of memory. They link together all of the terms, concepts and ideas you have stored from your experience. Frameworks operate on these associations in two ways:

1. They filter out all extraneous items not related to the contents of the framework. The sound of a clock ticking may bring to mind other associations such as time bombs, a count down for a space flight, "60 Minutes" or Geiger counters. Yet, the framework eliminates all of these irrelevant associations, because it contains only one kind of association and that is for "things that go bump in the night."
2. They classify items into specific

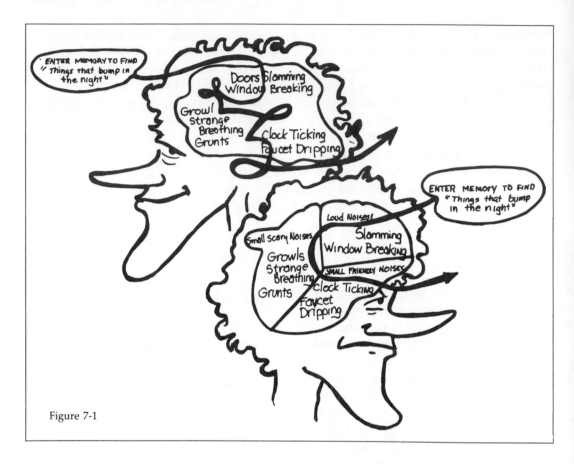

Figure 7-1

categories. Each item has a particular place or location. Therefore, a growling noise is not merely a thing that goes bump in the night, but more specifically, a small and scary thing.

Look at Figure 7-1. It represents how things that go bump in the night might be stored in your memory. The distances between the items correspond to their degree of association. The closer the items, the more associated they are in memory. Similar kinds of noises are clustered together. When you're asked to remember things that go bump in the night, and try to do so without an organizational framework, your recall process may look much like the path in the upper drawing. At best, it's a random exercise. You enter at an arbitrary point, and a group of sounds is recalled purely on the basis of association. One sound stimulates you to recall its closest associate. You wander through the structure from one association to the other until no more can be recalled. If you entered at another spot, say, "heavy breathing", you most likely would have produced a different list of sounds.

Now, contrast the above process with the recall procedure in the bottom cartoon. Here, your path is guided by the organizational map so you are sure to pass each specific category of noise. The categories, as well as the individual noises, are used to form associations.

So, pack new information in your mind with a handle that is readily reachable. Use an organizational or associational framework for they simplify and speed the memory process. If the material is familiar, you already have a framework, so use it. If the material is new, then use the ideas in this chapter to develop your own framework. And, if the material doesn't have an obvious structure or it consists of a list of words or numbers, then use linking systems or mnemonics.

Use elaboration techniques to link the material within your frameworks. Imagery skills are especially important in exaggeration, substitution and action techniques. The more bizarre the associations, the better.

How about "I forgot to remember"?

No, Nurf, you just didn't remember.

Chapter 8

Comprehension: Strategies

Putting Your Brain in High Gear

Such a request has probably gone through the mind of every student at one time or another, especially following exams. After all, when you can recite from memory the exact definitions and/or answers to questions concerning salient points in a course, it would seem you should be given at least a passing grade.

Not so. And the reason depends on the difference between memorizing a concept and understanding that concept as it applies generally. Students often feel well prepared for an exam only to discover they could not answer the questions because their preparation missed the kind of understanding the teacher was seeking.

And Dr. Snipegrabber may have underhandedly, unfairly and sneakily asked that his students demonstrate their understanding of a principle — which the students had memorized — by applying it to a situation never discussed in class. It's an unhappy and frustrating situation for both the student and the teacher, but it happens over and over again.

Let's go back to the major differences between good and poor learners. Remember we said poor learners do not have effective self-monitoring programs. Well, a second major difference is that poor learners often lack comprehension skills.

And that's what we're going to zero in on now. These skills are essential for understanding, rather than memorizing, new material. If you are to master new concepts or new conceptual material, these skills are mandatory. (And yes, you also have to have well developed self-monitoring skills to make any of these comprehension strategies work effectively.)

WARNING: Comprehension may be damaging to your rest habits.

It's going to be hard, probably some of the hardest mental work you'll ever do. It will require time, concentration and the use of many different strategies. But, it is the secret to a successful college career.

And, let's get something else clear. While IQ does have some relationship to comprehension ability, the most important variables are effective strategies, self-monitoring skills and laziness!

Good! At least I can qualify on one count. I'm rather proud of my superior self-development in that last area.

That's not quite the way I meant it, Nurt. Poor comprehension skills are often the result of people seeking the easy way out. As I've said, I'm much in favor of efficient and quick learning methods, but comprehension often demands effort and time. So what I'm going to offer you are strategies and a language for making the process as rapid and as meaningful as possible. Whereas you can be lazy in many learning tasks, comprehension demands that your brain be in high gear.

What does it all mean?

Comprehension is the "guts" of the learning process. It simply means understanding. And it goes far beyond books and examinations. One key to a successful life is the ability to understand your experiences whether they are based on books, TV, people, relationships or other situations you may encounter.

If you comprehend or understand an idea it usually means two things:

1. You are likely to remember it. Because it is "meaningfully" connected with your previous learning.
2. It probably has some generality. That is, it applies in other situations besides the one specific context in which it is presented.

Therefore, understanding the idea implies that you understand the more general principle or concept from which the specific example was derived.

Comprehension vs. memory

Many people say they don't like math or science or philosophy. Why? My guess is that the "real" reason is because dealing with concepts is difficult, and these three areas are full of concepts.

Conceptual learning is the hardest kind we encounter simply because you cannot memorize a concept. You must understand it as well. If you memorize without understanding, then you can apply the concept only in the specific instance you memorized. If you are asked on an examination to apply a concept to a completely new situation and you have just memorized the concept, then you are up a creek.

In my learning classes I have found that the majority of students can quickly improve their concentration and memory skills with a little practice. But comprehension is trickier for a rather improbable reason. Students often find it difficult to decide whether they do or do not actually understand the material! They simply don't know!

And they can thank the typical teaching methods employed in most high school and college classes for this unfortunate situation, for these classes usually require memorization rather than comprehension. Thus, the students develop learning strategies oriented toward memorization. When they come up against a class where genuine understanding is required, the result is BIG TROUBLE.

What's the big difference?

Let's take a look at the difference between memorization and understanding by looking at this Fenker F'r Instance.

> You're stopped at a red light over an intersection in a small town. You look in the rearview mirror and see a truck coming at you from behind at a high rate of speed with its horn blowing. You have two choices:
> 1. You can rely rigidly on the memorized traffic rule that "all vehicles must stop at a red light and assume that the truck will come to a screeching halt behind you. Or,
> 2. You can comprehend the actual situation, that the truck has lost its brakes, and run the red light before you are blasted into oblivion.

Now, from this example you can see there is some similarity between comprehension strategies and memory strategies. You did rely on your memory to tell you that trucks occasionally lose their brakes.

The problem, however, with this memorized rule or with any memorized information should be clear. Without comprehension, anything memorized becomes inflexible, specific and useless in novel situations. Memory strategies are most useful for learning information which stands alone with little connection to your previous learning.

Comprehension, on the other hand, is always a meaningful learning process. You either (1) understand the information quickly and easily because it fits with your previous knowledge, or (2) you change your knowledge by creating new categories of experience in order to understand. In both cases the material is not arbitrary; you either have an appropriate mental framework, or you create one.

Ah, ha, Fenker, I BELIEVE I Comprehend what you're saying. When I came to school I spotted this gorgeous gal walking out of the library. I made my move. But at that instant a cat about five-foot-twenty and two yards wide grabbed me by the arm and said, "Get lost. This is my chick. You dig?" I have not only memorized his words and concentrated on his size, but I have applied the concept to other situations. I do not speak to her in class, I do not tag her at the disco, I will cross the street to avoid meeting her when he is around. I do indeed dig!

That's it, Nurf. And "dig" is a fine definition of comprehension. You may live to a ripe old age because of your understanding of this situation.

What happens when you comprehend?

Okay, so we want to comprehend or understand. These are fine words, but also fairly vague and abstract. Let's try to narrow them down into concrete terms and look at some examples of strategies.

To begin, let's examine the different processes that comprehension involves.

1. **Expansion of your mental framework.** As we saw in Chapter 5, each of us has a mental framework for interpreting, classifying and making sense of the world around us. Comprehension often forces this framework to expand or change in some way. Imagine the following situation.

It's Aureola's first date with a sharp-looking guy she's been admiring for

months. He takes her to the Oilslick Tavern, a restaurant of questionable reputation and to her dismay, orders the house specialty, "Filet of Rocks", for each of them. Thirty, funfilled minutes later, the waiter appears with two oblong rocks cooked rare. Her date commences eating. What should she do? Everyone knows you don't eat rocks. Her choice is clear. Although at the moment her mental framework for food doesn't include the category "rocks", it's time she expanded it. The result? The beginning of a wonderful relationship bonded by the scrap-metal souffle and propane punch for dessert.

Don't be so flip about Aureola's experience. After all, we are still going steady.

Comprehension is the process of building mental frameworks which make meaningful learning possible. Comprehension strategies are, in fact, similar in many ways to memory strategies since both help you form associations or links between new and old material.

If you'll recall, memory links can be very bizarre and nonrealistic because the link's only purpose is to help connect two ideas in memory. For comprehension strategies, however, the nature of the links between the terms and ideas is often an important part of the knowledge you are attempting to understand.

If I asked you how an internal combustion engine works, you would need two types of knowledge to give a correct answer. First, you should know the basic parts — pistons, valves, cylinders, the carburetor. Second, you must understand how these parts are linked or related to one another.

You cannot comprehend the operation of the engine until you understand these links — that the explosions that drive the piston down the cylinder result from a mixture of air and gasoline being fired by the sparkplug.[1]

2. **Generalization.** Comprehension is a continual process of generalization. You first develop quite narrow mental frameworks for understanding the world and then, constantly expand or broaden them to fit new information. For example, let's take the concept of "reinforcement" as used in psychology. Many people consider reinforcement to be a kind of reward. "If you do thus and so I will give you a dollar or a car or a banana." This will reinforce what ever action you took. Any new rewards that fit the narrow category of "very pleasant events" will be understood as "reinforcements."

Yet, the true concept of reinforcement includes negative events such as shocks or

---

[1]Automotive scientists have found surprisingly that bronzed baby shoes hanging from the mirror, eight-track stereo systems and bumper stickers urging the election of Popeye play no part in the combustion process.

getting hit in the face with a pie. And it would also include secondary events with no obvious pleasant consequences — seeing a flash or hearing a buzzer. So, for an individual with a limited understanding of the term, "reinforcement," comprehension means expanding the original mental framework to include a variety of negative or neutral events.

3. **Organization.** Comprehension is also a process of organization. Your mind not only broadens (as in the previous example), but it also becomes more detailed and better organized. Can you remember when you were a child and all cars looked pretty much alike? Young kids usually divide highway vehicles into about three categories — cars, trucks and motorcycles. As they grow older, particularly when they reach their teens and want to own a car, the classification system becomes much more detailed and better organized.

These two kinds of changes go hand in hand. As your mental framework expands to include more cases or situations, it must become better organized to help you identify these cases. Thus, a Porsche gradually changes from being just a "small car" into a "fast, expensive, good-handling, well-made German sports car."

Surveys show that mothers of teen-aged daughters classify all vehicles into vans and non-vans (with good reason).

4. **Concept Learning.** As earlier defined, a concept is a rule or principle that applies to a variety of situations. Usually, concepts are presented in a particular context with a few specific examples. As a learner, your problem is to extract the underlying principle from these few examples and to be able to expand it to new and different situations.

You can learn a concept at two levels. You can memorize the definition and the examples and hope desperately the exam questions will ask you to either regurgitate the rules verbatim or recite one of the examples. This is the kind of memorized concept learning that is often confused by both teachers and students with genuine concept learning. Memorizing the concept doesn't mean you understand the concept.

The second level of concept learning involves comprehension. You understand the meaning of the concept in the sense that you can see (1) why it works in the particular examples you were given and (2) how it would apply in new situations. The better your comprehension, the further you can extend the concept beyond the original example to explain or solve new and different kinds of problems.

For instance, once you understand the simple principle of guiding a car with a steering wheel, you have mastered a concept which can be extended to other cars, trucks, buses, boats and even some airplanes.

If your instructors require only that you memorize concepts, take the next step and try to understand them. It will make your learning in the subject easier, and it can help you develop a powerful, expandable mental framework.

Keep active

One feature of all good comprehension strategies is activation. Each strategy is a method for insuring that your mind is actively involved in the learning task — that on your learning trip your transmission is in "drive", instead of "neutral" or "reverse."

This is necessary because comprehension is not a passive process. Your mind must be constantly perceiving, interpreting, associating new and old information, creating and expanding categories, generalizing and applying what you have learned to new situations.

This is called "thinking." And it's tough. Especially if your mind has gotten soft and lazy from disuse.

So now let's look at some exercises which will give your mental muscles a lit-

tle tone. I've stuffed your head full of a lot of information that was necessary before you could use it effectively. But now I promise you this: these strategies will be simple and straightforward, and you can use them immediately with very little practice.

But remember, your success will depend largely on the quality of your self-monitoring programs, so keep yourself on track and under control.

Comprehension Strategy No. 1: Paraphrasing

What's that? Well, if you do too much of it on a term paper, it's called plagarism or more bluntly, copying. Put properly, it's the process of restating, in your own terms, something you've heard or read. It would be stupid and a waste of time to try to restate everything, so paraphrasing is useful when you're not sure you understand what you're reading. Simple messages don't need further interpretation. "Get your hands off me," "Charles has a carrot in his ear," or "Apply to infected area," fall into this category. But in many books and classes, you're likely to encounter some of these problems:

• Writers who take several pages making a point that can be stated in a sentence or two.[1]
• Difficult vocabulary that appears to mask the meaning of the sentence.[2]

95

You mean that some people who write books use big words to impress the reader at the expense of making the sentence obscure, turgid, and non-understandable?

I'll ignore that.

• Conceptual statements that are difficult to understand when encountered for the first time or stated in someone else's terms.

This is where paraphrasing makes it easier to understand and remember the important substance of the material. Take a look at the following. First, read the sentence and try to paraphrase it before reading my own paraphrasing.

Antiquity and opulence form the crossroads of Turkey's past as the glowing red sun sets over the clear blue Mediterannean, ushering in twentieth-century technology. Jet planes, skyscrapers and electric toothbrushes tear gaping holes in the tranquil, agrarian Turkish history.

Now, you try it.

Here's my paraphrase: TURKEY IS ENTERING A NEW TECHNOLOGICAL ERA.

Let's try another:

Bob's excessive mastication resulted in a hypertrophic syndrome common to animals with ablations of the lateral hypothalamus.

Okay, your go.

Here's mine: BOB IS OVERWEIGHT.

Another: Evidence suggest that an Oedipus complex is an excellent predictor of homosexuality in males.

Your turn.

---

[1]Don't look at me, Dr. Fenker, I didn't say a word.
[2]Again, I didn't say a word.

Now, mine: MANY GAY MALES HAD EXTREMELY CLOSE RELATIONSHIPS WITH THEIR MOTHERS.

In the first example, one major point is pulled from the author's wordy statement. In the second, the material is stripped of its technological terminology. And in the third, the layman's wording is used for a complex psychological concept.

If you found your versions worded differently than mine, but with similar meaning, by George, you've got it! But if you had difficulty, we recommend you practice more familiar material with the help of a friend or teacher.

Here's how paraphrasing helps comprehension. If you directly restate a new idea in terms and concepts familiar to you, you've already gained some understanding of the idea. In your first attempts, the language should be simple and unambiguous. By using familiar terms you are guaranteed that the paraphrase will be associated with previous learning. You may be sacrificing generality, but this is of secondary importance if you're able to achieve some understanding of the idea.

As your understanding continues to increase, you will find your paraphrasing becomes more sophisticated. Many of the terms and concepts which at first seemed too technical or complicated will now be familiar to you.

Paraphrasing is a way to check your understanding of materials. If your comprehension of the subject is good, paraphrasing will be fairly easy. But if your understanding is only superficial and depends on terms not in your own language, then it becomes an almost impossible task.

For example, take the sentence "Her child-like narcissism made her behavior difficult to tolerate." You may think you understand it farily well; but, if you cannot clearly paraphrase the word "narcissism" (self-centered) you really don't understand what behaviors were objectionable.

Comprehension Strategy No. 2: Question-Answer

Simple. You formulate a question about the material and then try to answer it. But, the success of this strategy depends on how good you are at forming questions. When you've understood a topic fairly well, say football, it's usually easy to ask a question that illustrates your understanding.

Let's form a good question on football. (In case you're not a fan, here's your chance to practice your comprehension of a difficult and trivial subject).

"Why do linebackers weigh more than quarterbacks?" That's a good question because:

a. It reflects sufficient understanding of the subject to be relevant. The question implies that there might be a connection between the size of the player and his position or function.

b. It's phrased in such a way that answering it will increase your understanding of the subject. The use of such words as how, why or what insures the questions will have some explanatory power. Questions that can be answered with one or two words (yes, no, when, where) are generally less informative.

c. It has a meaningful answer. Questions that are vague (is football good?) or are categorically unanswerable (do ghosts like football?)[1] provide little information.

The Q/A technique is an excellent method for improving your comprehension skills because:

a. It's an active process that directs your attention to the important points in the material.

b. Once you have learned to ask yourself meaningful questions about a subject, it generalizes to many other tasks — class participation, exam taking and conversations. Plus, it's easier to predict what questions a teacher will ask.

c. It helps you identify which parts you do and do not understand.

It's good practice to ask questions which you can answer as well as those you can't. The latter tells you how much additional learning is necessary and where you need help. You'll find, too, that just by forming the question, your understanding of the subject is greatly increased.

One of the most important uses of the Q/A technique is to evaluate how you understand a concept or subject. In what sense do you understand it? Can you describe it, or explain it or relate it to something else? Knowing "how" you understand depends on having a language which expresses the kinds of understanding possible. And we'll hit that in the next chapter.

**Comprehension Strategy No. 3:
Playing teacher**

This method borrows skills from the previous two methods. Imagine that you have to explain the material to a friend.[2] And make your friend dumb — D-U-M-B! This means your explanations need to be clear and phrased in simple language. Also, assume that if you are uncertain about some parts of the material, these will be the very parts about which your friend will ask questions. Your friend has a fiendish streak and can always find where your understanding is weakest. (It would seem you do a poor job of choosing friends.)

Once you have created this simple-minded, but insightful friend, attempt to understand in his or her terms. Rehearse with yourself the explanations that you will give. If you encounter questions you

---

[1]The answer is "Yes." (See *The Galloping Ghost,* the biography of Red Grange.) Dr. Fenker, sometimes you use the worst examples.

[2] If you are unable to conjure up such a friend, then imagine talking to a class of brilliant students or to the blank wall of your choice.

cannot answer clearly, then get help from your teacher or from a real friend who knows what he or she is talking about.

I have found in my classes that this is an excellent technique for improving comprehension.

It's also helpful for students to practice by explaining difficult material to each other. This improves their examination and classroom performance by developing a sense of anticipation about questions which test understanding.

Comprehension Strategy No. 4: Doing it

This method applies especially well to material of a physical or concrete nature. The idea is to understand by translating concepts into imagined actions. Thus, in order to help understand why Force equals Mass times Acceleration, you might picture kicking a tin can or a basketball.[1] You will find it would take more force (from your kick) to cause the basketball to accelerate at the same rate as the can. By imagining how much of a kick is required in each case, you are translating the abstract physical law (f = ma) into concrete terms.

You might consider kicking a concrete block which would translate a physical law into a physical injury. Comprenez vous?

Oui, mon petit gamin. Psychological and sociological principles can often be learned this way. Instead of memorizing the abstract psychological law, apply the logic of this law to a familiar situation. For example, take the psychological principle, "Events which have been partially reinforced are very resistant to extinction."

What does that mean? Well, if you reward a dog with candy every time he stands on two legs, but then suddenly stop the rewards, the dog will break this habit fairly quickly. But if you give the dog candy only occasionally for this trick (partial reinforcement), he will persist long after the candy has stopped.

Now, can you see this principle at work in your own behavior? Some examples might be found in connection with pinball machines, most forms of gambling and many dating relationships.

Comprehension Strategy No. 5: Imagery

You see imagery techniques just about

---

[1]My memory circuits indicate that a football or a soccer ball would be an excellent example. But, then I suppose that would make too much sense for this chapter.

everywhere, don't you?[1] Well, they also apply to comprehension problems. Imagery is useful for understanding visual material that is difficult to explain verbally using paraphrasing or the Q/A techniques. For example, it's much easier to imagine a good golf swing than it is to describe such a swing with words, which might take a whole book. Imagery is also helpful in understanding how the parts of a problem or how the facts associated with a concept fit together to form a whole.

Comprehension Strategy No. 6: Organizing

Virtually all knowledge is highly organized regardless of its form — concepts, descriptions, terms. We've seen how this organization can be used to help memory processes. And now we find that a knowledge of organizational principles is vital for comprehension. Why? Because material seldom exists in isolation. It's part of a large collection of knowledge that is organized in some manner. Take the Civil War. It's only a small part of the history of the 19th century. And to be understood, we must have some familiarity with this earlier history.

When you are trying to understand new material, you are (1) learning about the specific properties of that material and (2) finding where that material fits into your organizational scheme for this type of information. For example, the connection between birds (specific material) and a zoological chart (organizational framework) is an important part of the knowledge necessary to understand zoology. And the process of fitting the parts into the chart is a comprehension strategy.

Authors, Ecch!

Now, I'll make you feel good about the problems you may have with some textbooks. When an author writes a book, he's obviously trying to share some knowledge with you. And in his mind that information is organized or linked together in some manner. Unfortunately, when it finally gets on paper, many of the author's goals and organizational plans can run together and become indistinct.[2]

When you read it, you may have trouble deciding just what the author had in mind. It is probably not your fault. Most textbook writers are not skilled in presenting information in ways that make it easy for you to understand. If they were more skilled, you would have to do little skimming, outlining or organizing on your own. In most cases, however, it is necessary for you to use these techniques to compensate for the writer's lack of clarity.[3]

---

[1] Well done, Dr. Fenker. You get three points for the clever juxtaposition of "see" and "imagery" in the same sentence. You are getting better as the book goes along.

[2] Come, Dr. Fenker, you're being too hard on yourself.

[3] Among such authors, Dr. Fenker is a legend in his own time.

Rewards of review

All of the above strategies apply to the review part of a study task. That is, you would use them after you had skimmed or read the material and were beginning to review it to improve your understanding.

How much time should you spend reading and rereading material as compared to reviewing it? Well, look at one of Fenker's Fascicles of Facts.

A number of college students were given a set of materials to learn. They were divided into five groups with each group instructed to use four hours of study in the following ways:

Group 1: four hours reading and re-reading the material
Group 2: three hours reading, one hour reviewing
Group 3: two hours reading, two hours reviewing
Group 4: one hour reading, three hours reviewing
Group 5: four hours, each student using his or her best method.

Results? You may be surprised. Group 4 performed the best on a test, closely followed by Group 3. Groups 2 and 5 were considerably poorer than the best groups and were followed by Group 1.

Significance: The majority of study time should be spent reviewing — that is — applying a comprehension strategy to the material you want to learn. Simply reading and rereading is not an efficient way to learn for most people.

Reading without reviewing and using a comprehension strategy is like traveling in low gear: You may eventually get there, but it'll take a long time. Comprehension methods engage the higher gears. They force your mental processes to be more effective. Finishing a chapter may represent the attainment of a practical goal, but without comprehension, you have not advanced much toward a learning destination. A comprehension strategy speeds you along the learning path.

What goal and when

Because complex subjects are tough, it may not be obvious that a comprehension strategy is succeeding. In fact, it may take months to actually understand the materials. You may be near the end of the semester before you really have a handle on the meaning and purpose of a class.

The reason is this: the signals that let you know "you are understanding something" are not always obvious. Often there are no immediate rewards, and that can make the whole task seem pretty brutal. Memory goals or specific work goals usually pay off quickly. But because comprehension goals are more difficult to achieve, you may not be able to see a destination clearly or even plan when you will arrive there.

Self-monitor or self-destruct

Here's where self-monitoring programs become all important. They are your tools for evaluating progress. Let's set up a self-monitoring scenario a good learner might use. (We'll assume that our learner has no difficulty with concentration. That much, we'll give him.)

Scene: A comfortable study area equipped with proper lighting, materials, etc. Student, wearing blue velvet smoking jacket, grey flannel trousers and an ascot foppishly arrayed around his neck, enters stage right and sits at desk.)

Student: Woe is me. This course in Nuclear Pistics sure is tough. I've been reading and concentrating well for the past 15 minutes, and I still don't understand the material.

(Light bulb on wire descends to just above the top of his head. An audible click is heard, and the light bulb goes on, signifying thought.)

Student: Ah Ha, It is probably time to apply one of Dr. Fenker's Fantastic Formulas to my problem — a Comprehension Strategy to help me understand. I'll attempt paraphrasing.

(Stage lights go off for ten seconds indicating the passage of 15 minutes. Lights go on.)

Student: Mercy, mercy! Even paraphrasing did not seem to help. There are too many technical terms for me to replace with appropriate substitutes. I am getting pale and wan in anticipation of the examination only two days hence. Clearly, I shall not be able to understand all of this pistics in so short a period. What shall I do?

(Light bulb descends again, clicks and goes on.)

Student: Ah Ha! I think I will attempt to develop an outline for this material. At least that will help me to remember the key items for the examination, the anticipation of which has me pale and wan.

(Stage lights go off indicating the

passage of another 15 minutes. Lights go on.)

Student: Glorioski! Organizing this technical junk into outline form has really helped me. I followed the author's chapter headings in developing my outline.[1] I am also beginning to see how each of the specific ideas relates to the whole chapter. Perhaps by exam time, I shall be able to understand. And I shall get my color back.

(Student stands as hook held by member of Actor's Equity reaches out from stage left and drags him off. A shot is heard. Curtain. No applause.)

Fenker, I had better lines when I played an eggplant in the first grade Food Pageant.

Okay, so I'm no playwright. But the above non-Pulitzer prize-winning scene does illustrate several major points in the application of self-monitoring techniques to comprehension.

Let's check them:

1. Your programs must be able to recognize situations in which reading, concentrating and memorizing are not getting the job done. At this point, you must act.
2. Shift to one of the specific Comprehension Strategies and note whether or not you are successful.
3. If not, shift to a more appropriate strategy.
4. If confronted with a deadline, an organizational strategy is most effective. Why? It helps develop a memory framework so you can at least recall the material even if you have not achieved a good understanding.

Yes, do you know where I can buy a good book on comprehension?

I don't understand the question.

---

[1] Ahem, Dr. Fenker. You see some authors can present their materials in a logical manner.

Chapter 9

The Language of Comprehension

"How do I understand thee? Let me count the ways . . ."

I'm not one of those "Mr. Fixit" people. I even have trouble putting in a new light bulb. And when I lift the hood of my car, I might as well be deep in the interior of the Brazilian jungle as far as recognizing anything familiar. Not too long ago, I was driving down the highway when my car's engine began to falter. I managed to nurse it into a garage a couple of miles down the road and finally located a mechanic who was elbow deep into a torndown engine. I tried to describe my problem, pointing out that something in the engine started wheezing and sputtering. Next, the whole thing began vibrating and shaking and finally slowed down.

He peered into the hood a couple of minutes and said something like, "Well, you got problems. Looks like the revolving shaftspleen on the distributor assembly has fractured, throwing it out of alignment which then caused an oscillating resonance that led to the collapse of the gascolator screen which forced ferrous particles up through the carburetor diaphragm, resulting in an improper fuel-air ratio that brought you down on the back side of the power curve."

I stood, stunned, for a moment and then asked him what all that meant.

He pulled the toothpick out of his mouth and said, "Who knows? But, that's why it will be so expensive to fix."

Fenker, you're lying through your hollow teeth. You know that conversation never took place.

Well, it may not have been word for word, but the result was the same. I didn't know what he was talking about, and he took me for about 85 bucks.

The point is: he was using language that I didn't understand. And that left me clear out in left field. He might have just as well been speaking Urdu. And therein lies the problem that many students run into in class. The teacher often uses a language of comprehension that they may only partially understand.

For example, here's a conversation that has happened many times between teachers and students.

> **Student:** Look, I studied and studied for this exam, and I knew the material inside out, but I got a lousy 35. Now, here's a question I know was answered right, and you marked it wrong.
>
> **Teacher:** The question was, "Compare the great Pigmy rebellion during the summer of '42 to the riot at

the Chelsey Square Station in '66 when the Beatles got off the train wearing Nehru jackets." You described the rebellion in gory detail. Then, you also described the Beatles' riot. But I asked you to compare these events. I can't tell from your answer if you really understood the two events since you didn't identify their similarities or differences."

And this is where the language of comprehension comes in. The language contains the words that refer to the kinds of understanding you are expected to have — words such as define, compare, organize, explain the consequences or identify.

When my car broke down, I badly needed to know its special language — pitted points, clogged carburetor, slipping clutch. Why? Because the words in this special diagnostic language let me describe to a mechanic specifically what needs to be fixed. In short, it is a set of tools for translating vague, general statements about the car (it's making a noise) into precise and concrete statements about what needs to be fixed (the valves need adjusting.)

I don't get it??

In a similar way, a language of comprehension permits you to translate vague statements such as "It doesn't make any sense," into specific statements such as "I can describe the parts of a cell, but I can't locate or organize them." Or, "Measles and mumps are both classified as childhood diseases, but I can't compare their causes." Or, "I don't know what the consequences would be of living in a very noisy environment."

A language of comprehension is, therefore, useful for monitoring your own learning activities as well as for helping you communicate with a teacher or a friend.

Do you understand "Understanding?"

1. **Describe it.** It's a big box with a glass viewing screen on one end next to a bunch of knobs and has an electric cord and a bunch of holes on the other end.

2. **Define it.** It's a device for receiving electromagnetic waves and turning them into images on a screen.

3. **Paraphrase it.** It's often called a "boob tube."

4. **Classify it.** It's one of many electron-

ic devices for home entertainment and communication. Others include radios, stereos, tape decks and slide projectors.

5. **Organize it.** It's made up of three sections: parts that include the frame, back and other supporting units; parts that receive and amplify the signals from the station; and parts that transform the signals into pictures on the screen.

6. **Compare it.** It's much more complicated and expensive than a radio.

7. **Note its influence on something.** Its entertainment value causes many people who might otherwise go out to stay home.

8. **Note something's influence on it.** Low-flying planes often interfere with the picture quality.

9. **Give evidence or arguments for it.** It's a powerful educational tool as well as a medium for entertainment.

These are common types of understanding. But what is important is that these terms are "operational." Each describes a specific thing you can do to develop or test your understanding. Some of you with greasy fingernails have many types of understanding for automobiles, but if I say "nuclear power generator" you probably couldn't express your understanding in as many ways as before.

However, the comprehension language we've just described can help you decide in what specific ways your understanding is limited. And this is a good place to start in becoming an effective learner.

Pick your own language

My students liked the idea of using a "language of understanding," but often they couldn't make it work, because some of my terms weren't appropriate for them. They had a good point. The list above isn't unique. There are many ways of describing, organizing, comparing, and so forth.

So here are some additional terms that are associated with these nine categories. You may find some fit your comprehension language better than those I have used.

1. **Describe**
   Give a description
   Characterize
   Label
   Elaborate
   Identify parts, features,
     attributes, components
2. **Define**
   Give a definition
   Explain
   Identify
   Understand the meaning of
   Analyze
3. **Classify**
   Fit into a classification
     scheme
   Note what it is a part of
   Categorize
   Identify as a member of
     a group, family, subset
     or organization.
4. **Paraphrase**
   Restate

Put into different words
Repeat something in your
  own language
Articulate
5. **Compare**
Contrast
Relate
Examine both sides
Discriminate
Form analogies
Find similarities or
  differences
Express the relationship
  between things in time
  or space
6. **Organize**
Identify the basic structure
Divide into classes or
  categories
Diagram
Relate the parts in some
  orderly way
Put the parts together
7. **Can Influence Something**
Leads to
Can have an effect on
Is the cause or partial
  cause of some result
Is to produce a change
Is to express an inter-
  action between two things
Is to see a cause-effect
  relationship
8. **To be Influenced by Something**
Is to be affected by
  something
Is to see how a cause
  produced a particular

effect
Is to see the result of
  an action
Is to note the consequences
Is to see forces operating
  that produce an end result
9. **Citing Evidence**
Present supporting data
  for
Provide relevant informa-
  tion
Offer favorable arguments
Demonstrate the logic
  of a position
Give rationale for
Refute counter-arguments
Rule out contradictory
  information

Sometimes your intuition will tell you that you do or don't understand something. But, you still need to communicate your degree of understanding. The terms above form a "language" for describing how well you understand. And this language helps you avoid situations where you know you don't understand, but can't decide why or what you should do about it.

Okay, Fenker, I'll play the straight man. Now that I've got a zillion terms, and you have deeply impressed me as to how valuable they will be, how do I talk "comprehension?"

I thank you for setting up this next section, Nurf. I'll be happy to give you a lesson in basic *LARC*. That's an acronym for "Language for Rapid Comprehension." I'm going to give you a couple of scenarios in which a good learner has a conversation with himself or herself about a comprehension problem. Notice how speaking LARC keeps the conversation meaningful and specific. It eliminates much of the vagueness and uncertainty often associated with understanding problems.

Fenker's Famous Case of The Uncommunicative Teacher or What the Heck Does She Want?

Setting: New class, new teacher. The student realizes the lowest level of comprehension involves direct memorization of items. But he suspects the teacher wants him to develop a deeper understanding of the subject. He is faced with the problem of deciding just what kinds of understanding the teacher considers important. We tune in on his self-talk.

"I was an idiot to sign up for this course on the History of the 16th Century Lower Grainola. It looked like a sure "A" or "B" at worst. But this lady is weird — she expects us to learn something. She keeps using Lower Grainolian history to draw conclusions about current day events. Well, I'd better get at it. But, before I waste a lot of time reading the material, I need to decide what

kinds of understanding she expects. And I'd better start talking in *LARC* to keep my thinking concrete.

First, she expects us to see similarities between Lower Grainolian events and current events. This is probably understanding by comparison or analogy. I might list Lower Grainolian events (shouldn't take long, its history only has four events which is why I thought this course would be a snap) in one column and current events in another. Then, I'll see if they have any similarities or points in common. Now, is there any other kind of understanding required?

Well, we were supposed to discuss the influence of Lower Grainolian history on current events. This may be tough because the world has totally ignored their history. There was the time their King, Bruce the Bald, underwent the first hair transplant in history. During a heavy rain it slipped down, producing a beard with a cowlick. But, that's the only influence the Lower Grainolians have ever had."

Fenker's Famous Case of The Seemingly Ambiguous Textbook or What Does It Really Say?

Setting: New book, no instructor. The student has no help as to the kinds of understanding he is expected to have. He knows that most books provide abundant clues which communicate the important kinds of understanding. His problem is to learn to recognize these clues and use them to direct his study.

"This sociology book is stupid. It has nothing but one case history after another. Some are interesting, but what am I suppose to learn from all this? It would be ridiculous to try to memorize it (although my memory is now finely tuned, thanks to Good Dr. Fenker's Chapter 7). Perhaps the text contains some clues to help me decide what to understand. Why does the author present these cases? Well, they're organized into short chapters, and at the start of each chapter, there's a fairly broad statement which represents what the author believes is true. Ah, ha! Quel

Stupide! The title of each chapter is simply a version of the statement describing the chapter's purpose.

For example, the title of Chapter 5 is, "Gangs as Substitute Families." And the introductory discussion suggests that in many respects a street gang will provide a number of the needs such as discipline, companionship and affection normally associated with a family group.

Now what kind of understanding does the chapter communicate? Each of the cases represents evidence for the author's theories. I can learn what kind of evidence each case represents and organize the information. Then, I won't have to remember the specific details of each case. Thus, the chapter contains three cases illustrating how gang discipline substitutes for parental control. That's the kind of understanding the author wants to communicate."

I've been framed, luckily

A few chapters back we saw that both efficient memory processes and comprehension depend on developing association frameworks. They represent a type of organizational chart which summarizes the key facts or ideas. The major parts (or nodes) of such frameworks are linked in many ways. For memory tasks, it's enough just to know that several terms are associated — cars, tires, windshields. For comprehension tasks, however, the nature or types of links are very important. To see how important, read this fable.

A Formidable Fenker Fantasy

Grosselda, who was raised in the wilderness by snarks until the age of 16, is captured by natives, sold to an animal dealer and arrives in this country in a shipment of tone-deaf sloths. You find her in a petshop window on special with a free leash and flea collar. Never one to regret a bargain, you bring her home and begin her education. Gradually, she picks up a few words — car, engine, bumper, and wheels. She learns

they are associated. Thus, her memory framework might look like Figure 9-1. The circles represent the nodes, the parts of the car she remembers. The links, the lines connecting the nodes, are completely arbitrary because she does not know how they are associated.

After threatening her with whip and chair, she finally learns that these words are parts of a car. And thus, the links in her memory framework become meaningful, and the framework becomes useful for understanding, not just remembering. These frameworks with meaningful links are called networks.[1] Now, that she has learned which

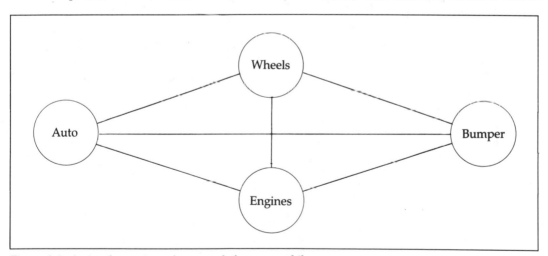

Figure 9-1. A simple memory framework for automobile.

[1]Dr. Fenker is exercising his penchant for pedantry. He uses the term networks to describe frameworks used for comprehension. He says he does this to stress the fact that for understanding, the links must be meaningful. Whereas, in an association framework, the links can or cannot have meaning. He is a pain.

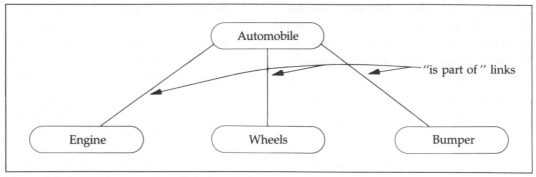

Figure 9-2. A simple network with links which represent "is a part of."

things are "parts of" a car, her network will look like Figure 9-2.

Finally, after depriving her for five days of her favorite food, refried parsnips under plastic, she finally understood the relationship between the parts. Now, there are many types of links, both simple and complicated, which express the relationships of the parts to the concept "car." And her network now looks like Figure 9-3. We can see how a typical network quickly becomes complicated as each new bit of experience or information adds links to the whole.

Grosselda recently married a self-employed postman and became president of General Motors.

That's a fascinating story, Fenker. It must be wonderful to be a famous author and get to hobnob with such interesting people.

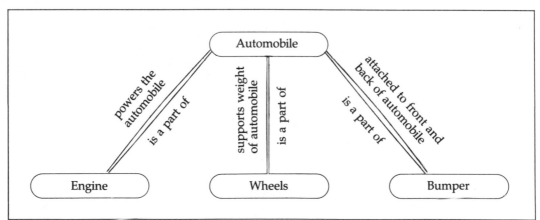

Figure 9-3. A more complicated network with several types of links.

Gives you something to shoot for, doesn't it, Nurf. But, I shared this very personal experience with you to point out that much classroom learning proceeds in just such a manner. When you first study a new subject, you may spend most of your time memorizing terms or definitions without really understanding how they are tied together. As the course progresses, you learn how various terms and concepts are connected, and you develop new links in your network for that subject. These links are the glue that allows you to build and hold together complicated networks of knowledge.

Links and LARC

There are an infinite number of possible relationships among the nodes of a network. But the most likely ones were given earlier in this chapter in describing the comprehension language, LARC.

Anytime you can ask a question which improves your understanding, you're adding a new link to your network. Such questions include:

• What is it a part of?
• What does it influence?
• What influences it?

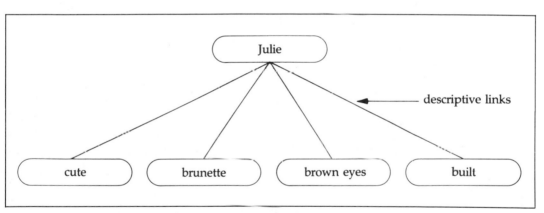

Figure 9-4. A discriptive network.

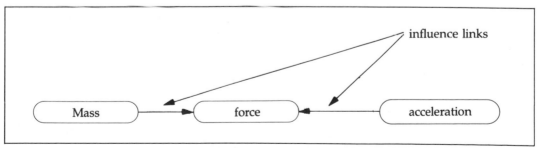

Figure 9-5. A simple conceptual network.

• How do you describe it?
• What does it compare to?

For example, a simple descriptive network might look like Figure 9-4. A conceptual network could look like Figure 9-5. Figure 9-6 illustrates another network showing organization or classification.

As your knowledge of a subject increases, a few abstract links may replace a large number of specific links. Thus, in an early network for cars, you might list many "parts." But, a later network would sort them into categories such as "body parts" and "engine parts."

So to review: Comprehension depends on building mental networks in which terms, ideas or concepts are linked in some manner. And the links define how each pair of items is related.

Networks and speed learning

The subjects we are familiar with —

sports, cars, friends, even basic math or English — are probably organized into fairly complicated networks. But the problem facing many learners is that of building networks for new areas. It can be a slow haphazard process. First, facts are memorized. Gradually, the appropriate links develop. Finally, a high quality network is formed.

I have just dipped into my six-pack of foresight and have quaffed deeply. Fenker, why go clear around Robin Hood's barn to get there? Why not just put the material we want to understand directly into network form? Thus, eliminating the middle man and his markup?

Quel manifique, Nurf. That's a great question.[1] You can do just that. You can eliminate some of those intermediate steps between memorizing and understanding.

As you read, study, underline, listen to lectures, take notes or use any of the com-

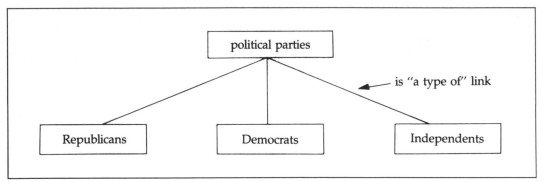

Figure 9-6. A classification network.

[1]"Great question" is Dr. Fenker's ploy for handling a question he can't answer.

prehension strategies we've suggested, you can systematically attempt to construct networks at the same time. And there's another side-benefit. Once you have developed a network, almost no effort is required to remember it!

For example, memorize this sentence:

"Dises Mädchen geht abends oft auf den Strich."

Rough?

Okay, contrast it with this:

"That girl often walks the streets at night."[1]

Easy? English is your language, not German. You have a "network" for English, thus, it is easily remembered. Understanding is built into the structure of a comprehension network just as understanding comes from reading the English sentence.

Building a better mousetrap

Let's tackle the big problem of constructing a comprehension network for new or difficult material. Here's how you go about it:

1. **Explore or leave trail markers.** The first time you explore new material, keep your gun at ready and pass through fairly quickly. Don't get bogged down with details or difficult passages. Be alert to note important features of the terrain — the im-portant points in your text material. Underline, highlight or mark in some way the ideas, concepts or terms you think are important. Also, mark those you don't understand clearly with a special notation such as a question mark.

2. **Review and elaborate.** List all the terms or concepts you underlined on the left hand side of a piece of paper. Then, re-read the passage more carefully, paying special attention to the underlined terms. If you learned anything new about them or how they relate to each other, make a note of this in the margin as you read. For example, if you find the words "reinforce-ment" and "reward" are used inter-changeably, make a note of this in the right hand column. If you find a definition for a term you didn't understand, jot it down in the right hand column. As an ex-plorer, you are now organizing informa-tion on all the important terrain features.

3. **Construct a map or network.** Orga-nize as many of the terms or concepts as possible into a "terrain map" or network. Place the terms that are closely related near each other. Next, draw lines between those terms that are linked together in im-portant ways. Then, label the links that connect them. If you're not sure how they are related, research the relevant parts for information or ask someone.

It's easier to understand a difficult sub-ject if you do it part by part. You have a better chance of getting useful information when you ask about specific nodes and

---

[1]Dr. Fenker contends she is just an old family friend. He's so transparent!

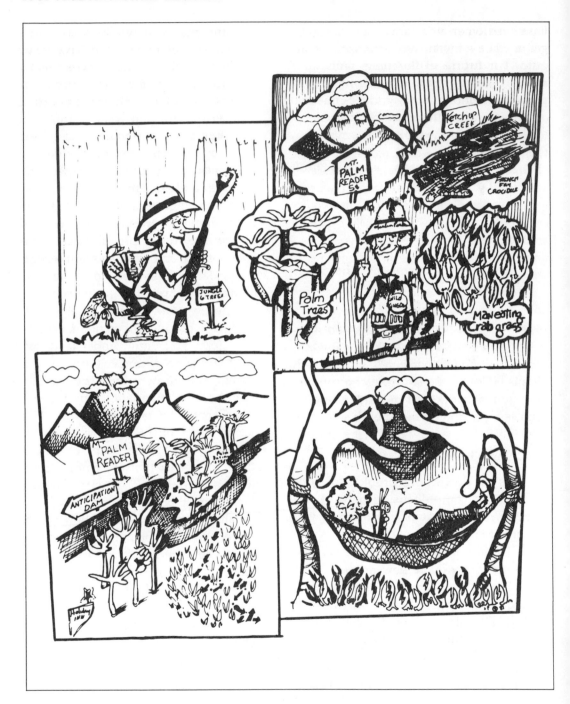

links than when you simply say "I don't get it." The network will now serve as a guide for future explorations with the same material. And, it will provide a powerful memory framework to help you at test time when the map isn't available.

There will always be a few familiar terms or concepts which represent your "home base." Try to increase your understanding by relating these familiar terms to unfamiliar ones. You'll find that your circle of knowledge will gradually expand around these familiar terms as you continue to make new links in a larger network.

4. **Relax.** You've really got it made now. Once you've built your network, you'll be surprised at how much more you understand about the material. It will now be easier to add new concepts or to tie all sorts of specific facts and details to it. And when it comes to exams, your preparation may need to involve little more than reviewing the network and asking yourself about possible links you may have omitted.

Let's do it

Let's build a network from the following passage:

As a member of a scientific expedition traveling through the unexplored equatorial rain forest of the Central Range of the Malay Peninsula in 1935, I was introduced to an isolated tribe of jungle folk, who employed methods of psychology and inter-personal relations so astonishing that they might have come from another planet. These people, the Senoi, lived in long community houses, skillfully constructed of bamboo, rattan, and thatch, and held away from the ground on poles. They maintained themselves by practicing dryland, shifting agriculture, and by hunting and fishing. Their language, partly Indonesian and partly Neo-Kamian, related them to the peoples of Indonesia to the south and west, and to the Highlanders of Indo-China and Burma, as do their physical characteristics.

Study of their political and social organization indicates that the political authority in their communities was originally in the hands of the oldest members of patrilineal clans, somewhat as in the social structure of China and other parts of the world. But, the major authority in all their communities is now held by their primitive psychologists whom they call *halaks*. The only honorary title in the society is that of *tohat*, which is equivalent to a doctor, who is both a healer and an educator, in our terms.

How did it go? Here's what I underlined?

Live on the Malay Peninsula

117

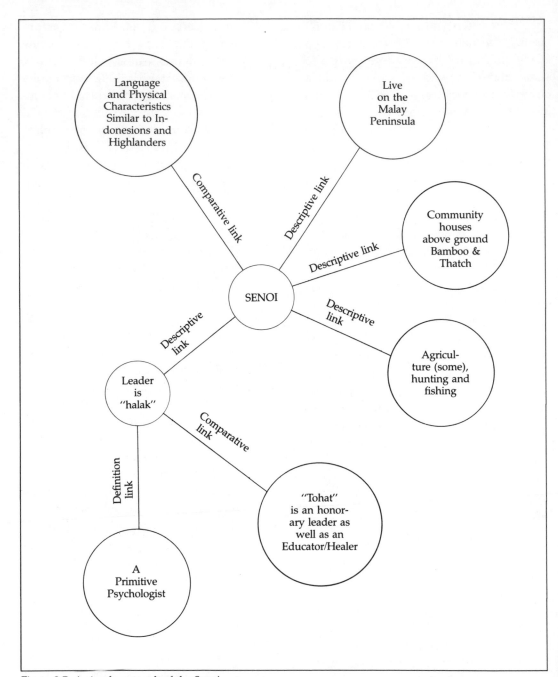

Figure 9-7. A simple network of the Senoi.

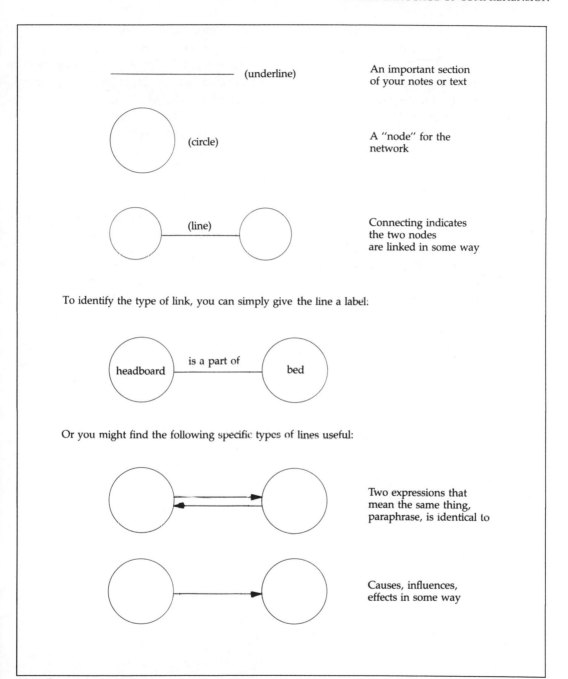

Figure 9-8. Graphic symbols useful in note-taking.

Community houses above the ground, made of bamboo and thatch

Limited agriculture, hunting, fishing

Language and physical characteristics similar to Indonesians and Highlanders

Leader is *"halak,"* a type of psychologist

Honorary leader is *"tohat,"* educator, healer.

The next step is to organize these key terms into a network. Since they all relate to the Senoi, this term becomes the central node. Figure 9-7 illustrates this network. If you have a great deal of material to cover, your network might not be this detailed. If your material is more difficult, you can make additional passes to better define or elaborate the nodes.

One more thing that may help you is having a few graphic symbols to use in note taking and studying. You might consider my network shorthand system as illustrated in Figure 9-8.

Only one thing that I'm not sure of — that guy Tohat who was mentioned in the article. Think I knew him. Did he go to John Wilkes Booth Junior High?

No, Nurf, he was a senator from South Carolina who helped resurrect the post-Civil War South by gaining passage of a law requiring little tufts of cotton to be placed in aspirin bottles.

Chapter 10

Problem Solving

Life Is Just One Problem After Another

"Houston, we have a problem!"

Those words, crackling ominously over two hundred thousand miles of space from the command module of Apollo 13, triggered one of the most intense, massive, concentrated problem solving exercises in the history of mankind. An explosion of one of the oxygen tanks had left the three crewmen in a position never before experienced by members of the human race — being stranded forever away from their own planet.

Literally hundreds of scientists, technicians, specialists and experts in dozens of disciplines pitted their skills of learning, memory, comprehension, concentration, and creativity against a life-or-death situation in a pitifully short time frame. But, as in the good old fashioned westerns, the cavalry came galloping over the horizon just in the nick of time to save the wagon train. Our latter day trooper-scientists plotted a new sequence of actions that brought our astronauts home safely.

When we say "problem" we too often think in terms of something being "wrong" as in Apollo 13. Wrong. Let's face it. Life is nothing more than a never-ending sequence of problems. And, problem solving is nothing more than taking the initiative to reach a particular objective. And until you obtain that objective

(or give up trying), it represents a problem. So, in this context, problem solving becomes the process of getting what you want out of life. And problem solving skills become the tools to help you do it.

Successful learning isn't enough

By now you should be well on your way to becoming a more effective learner. We're now turning to problem solving because successful learning doesn't depend simply on memorizing, concentrating or comprehending. Instead, it demands your ability to apply your learning to solve a particular problem.

Laboratory classes come to mind. They often require that you apply your understanding of a subject to solve elementary problems. On the job training, from garbage collection to college teaching, asks you to apply certain knowledge to the performance of your job. And, it probably will be knowledge not learned in school.

Let's examine problem solving further. It is the act of putting into practice ideas or learned skills to reach a particular objective. It is doing rather than thinking, worrying, anticipating and planning, although it normally will involve all these activities. It is a traveling process with many possible paths. Some reach the destination;

others don't. And the success of your problem solving efforts depends on your ability to navigate among the many possible solutions and select a path that leads to your chosen destination.

Like comprehension, problem solving is an activity which may take considerable time simply because you cannot always force a solution to appear. Therefore, it is essential for you to focus on the process or technique of problem solving. A good process, what you actually do when you attempt to solve a problem, will always move you in the direction of a solution.

To someone without adequate skills in this area, problem solving can be a series of nightmares. Some people try to avoid problem solving by developing a life style that ignores problems altogether! But this never works, for life is a continued series of school problems, social problems, work problems, money problems, ad infinitum.

Who asked for it?

If that weren't enough, many of our problems are not of our own making. For example, your parents may want you to become a doctor. But, you have your heart set on being a lawyer.

As a student, an employee or even a member of society, you cannot avoid such dilemmas. Often, you must solve problems someone else has created in order to reach your own objectives. The terrible truth is that most jobs are based exactly on this principle. That's what people get paid for doing.

But problem solving is goal seeking. And this is the essence of a self-fulfilling life. You can't sidestep problems; you can only fool yourself by not facing them or refusing to acknowledge what the real problem is.

So, ol' Fenker is going to see to it that you're armed with the skills to deal with personal, academic, and work-related problems. These skills will help translate your memory, concentration and comprehension abilities into action. And action is the name of the game.

Problem solved? Well . . .

Before we plow any deeper into this matter, let me caution you about the use of the word "solved." It has a beautiful cut-and-dried finality about it. Problem solved, the sun shines and all's right with the world. Right? Wrong, again.

Many problems, in particular real life problems, are never solved. More often they're resolved. Problems such as getting a friend into a steady dating relationship. Or, trying to make a cantankerous 70 year-old grandmother happy about living alone. Real problems. They're problems that might be solved, but they are more likely to be resolved. Why? Because the outcome depends on others.

The dating arrangement may not work out (the solution may be breaking up). You might not get the job you want. Or your grandmother may never be happy alone. In each case, the preferred solution may not be feasible, because it depends on someone else's agreement. Often a compromise or other form of resolution must be achieved in order to end an unpleasant dilemma.

Fenker, you have a problem! So far, you've spent four pages telling us how important it is to solve problems — but without a single word of advice on how to do it. To throw your non-specific words back in your curiously arranged teeth, "You can't avoid it, and action's the name of the game."

Touché, Nurf. But at the risk of sounding as if I'm hedging, there's nothing that will transform you from an ordinary student to a dynamic super-solver able to leap large obstacles with a single solution. The best I can offer is a problem solving technique. It will work well on many types of obstacles if you'll recognize that problem solving is no guaranteed quick process. It often takes considerable time to even bring the real problem into focus.

It's FAST but sort of slow

It's FAST — Fenker's Awesome Solution Technique. But it's slow in that it involves taking a number of steps in the proper sequence and completing each one before proceeding. Let's start with you selecting one of your current problems and deciding where you are in this sequence. Then, attempt to apply the remaining steps to

reach the problem's solution.

STEP 1. Accept responsibility for the problem.

Unless you're willing to acknowledge that the problem is your responsibility (or that you're willing to make it your responsibility), forget it. Just admit that you're not willing to take on the problem or recognize that it has no solution and quit worrying about it. In other words, either take the problem solving situation seriously or don't take it at all. Front and center or back of the bus.

Problems seldom resolve themselves. They're usually resolved by action (people taking responsibilities and acting on them) or by inaction (maintaining the status quo by doing nothing). But, remember this: You are just as responsible for any inaction as for a particular course of action. Ignoring a problem doesn't relieve you of responsibility for the problem.

Why is accepting responsibility the most important first step? For the same reason that the first step required of a person joining Alcoholics Anonymous is to admit that he or she is an alcoholic. A poor learner often finds it difficult to improve because he refuses to accept the responsibility for his difficulties. Such a person might tell himself "I didn't want to come to school," or "I don't care anything about this subject," or "It's useless to study; the teacher has it in for me," or finally, "It's a waste of time to study for this exam since grades really don't mean anything to me."[1]

Such excuses attempt to place the responsibility for your lack of interest in learning on someone or something other than yourself — parents, teachers, subjects, school, friends, famine, disease, pestilence and/or war.

Few students like every subject they take. Even fewer like examinations on these subjects. Yet, most do well in college. Why? Because they don't let their reasons for being at school influence how much they learn. They accept the responsibility for what happens. It doesn't matter whether you're in school to please your parents, to start a career, to learn or to make friends. What happens is still your responsibility.

STEP 2. Examine the problem and collect information.

This simply means finding what the problem is all about. You'll usually be surprised at how little you know (or acknowledge you know) about it. Information can come from your own experiences, or from friends, books or experts in the problem area. You may well find yourself returning over and over to this stage as you will continually be receiving new information.

How do you learn more about it? Well, you might need to break it down into small parts and see how they interrelate or relate to the whole problem. You may need to compare it with similar situations, deciding where they are alike and where they are different. You may want to see what other people have done in similar situations. And finally, you may need to ask questions to determine the real problem.

There is no right way to examine a problem. You'll have to decide what works best for you. But at this stage, don't

---

[1]For additional examples, send for our 28.48 pound compendium of "The Twenty-Eight Thousand, Four Hundred and Eighty Great Excuses of Our Time." $28.48. Freight and handling charge: $28.48.

try to solve it! Considering a possible solution may foul things up. It may restrict your information-gathering efforts or keep you from considering all possible alternatives. At this stage, focus on collecting information, analyzing and asking questions.

STEP 3. Define the problem

The best way to solve a problem is to discover during the first two steps that the original problem doesn't really exist! The real problem is often not what you originally thought. The purpose of defining the problem is to see if the original problem has changed, or if it needs redefining. When you started to work on the problem, you began with a basic definition. As you thought about the problem and collected information, your understanding increased. Each restatement or redefinition of the problem moved you closer to the truth. Finally, you gained some insight into the "true" problem.

Thanks a lot! I'm finally getting into specifics, and now you throw in this nebulous curve called insight. Where do I pick up the large economy box of that? If I had insight, I probably wouldn't need this book in the first place.

Insight is a special kind of skill that enables us to solve problems by "seeing" them from a different perspective. A fox, frustrated by a high wall separating him from the chicken yard, has an insight when he discovers he need only go around the wall, not over it. Each time you restate the problem in clearer, more correct terms you are achieving new insights.

Take the case of Absent Abigail. She hates to go to class in the morning. In fact, she has missed most of her classes before noon. Her first analysis goes like this: "My morning classes are boring, and I'm often sleepy because I stayed up late the night before."

She decides to collect some new information. And, to her surprise, things change. She finds (a) she dreads going to class because her grades are poor, she doesn't participate in discussions, and she's embarrassed for appearing stupid; and, (b) the classes are not all boring. In fact, two of them are among her favorite subjects.

Now, when she takes another shot at a better definition of the problem, she will focus on her unhappy experiences in the classroom rather than the more superficial issues of "staying up late" or "boring subjects." Staying up late may still be a part of the problem that needs to be solved. It may be that she stays up late because she isn't planning on going to class anyway.

Hold it, Fenker. You listed as Step 2, collecting and analyzing information, and

Step 3, as redefining the problem. And you also said we must take these steps in the proper sequence. Now you're getting them all mixed up — going back and forth from one to the other.

Guilty, as charged, Nurf. Although problem definition is listed as the third step in the process and "collecting and analyzing information" is the second step, these activities actually occur simultaneously, and so do the remaining activities described below. Think of the problem solving process as a sequence of events, but also as a series of feedback loops where each stage feeds simultaneously into the other stages.

When you have completed the definition stage, you should have in hand a clear statement of what you think the problem means. This definition commits you to a particular plan of action, because it acts as a "filter" for your future descriptions of the problem. Now, at some later time, you may need a totally new definition. So don't be afraid to throw it all out, change your mind and start over. I told you this was a process that couldn't be rushed.

Cat Skinning — Let me count the ways.

There are many methods for defining a problem. Here are some ways that might bear fruit.[1] Your definition of the problem may be:

a. Your concept or attitude about the problem.
b. The truth as far as you know it at the time.
c. Your current understanding of the problem.
d. Your clearest intention, your ultimate goal.
e. Your expectations.
f. Your title for the problem.

STEP 4. Generate ideas for solving the problem.

Now that you've defined it, it's time to come up with some ideas for a solution. Warning: beware of your favorite ideas. Ideas are paths that carry your thinking and actions in certain directions. Many of these paths will be deadends. Others may get you to a solution only after a long and tortured process. So, choose the ideas that are related to your objectives rather than trying to alter your objectives to fit a great sounding idea.

Ideas are cheap; they're dime a dozen until they are focused on a particular objective and put into action. Your first goal, then, is to generate a great number of ideas. The more ideas, the better your chances of ending up with a winner.

---

[1]Fenker just plain lifted this list from an excellent book by Don Koberg and Jim Bagnall called the *Universal Traveler*. He tried to improve on it, but failed, I presume he just couldn't define his problem well enough.

Here are some idea generators that will turn out several bagfulls of alternative thoughts:

Brainstorming. In this technique, used by small groups, ideas are quickly and freely contributed by everyone according to the following guidelines:

1. Do not criticize any ideas at this stage.
2. Be loose; let your mind wander in any direction, particularly to the unusual, the strange and the bizarre.
3. Don't wait for a novel idea to appear. Tag on or hitchhike on the last idea given.
4. Go for quantity rather than quality. You can sort them out later.

Manipulative Verbs. Select verbs that change a problem's perspective — magnify, minify, substitute, reverse, invert, combine, divide, separate, rotate, repeat, abstract, thicken, etc. For example, by reversing the plot of "The Perils of Pauline" you might have the heroine, Pauline, taking advantage of the villain, and the tall dark stranger could be gay.

Analogies. This forces the problem to relate to some other subject or situation. Then the attributes of that other object or situation may give you some new ideas about the original problem. For example, assume you were designing an environmentally based home. You might compare the home to an animal such as a bear or fox. One attribute of these animals is their protective fur coats that change thickness with the season. Therefore, a house covered with a plant that is thick and insulating in winter and light and airy in summer might work.

STEP 5. Choose a plan of action.

Now that you've decided what constitutes the real problem and have generated a list of possible ideas for a solution, select one as a plan of action. That's the key: action. You want the plan that represents the best solution. But which is best? There's no guaranteed answer. And there are many situations where you will not be able to reach a clear decision. *BUT, DO SOMETHING!* Choose one of the ideas. Even if it turns out to be the second or third best, putting it into action is an excellent way to discover this fact.

Don't worry about not choosing the best one first. Few decisions are irreversible. You normally will have the chance to correct a bad decision. And, the consequences of not acting are often worse than if you make the wrong choice. Why? Because if you don't act, you're letting someone else or the "circumstances" make decisions for you. To be undecided about whether to study English or geography and resolve this problem by studying neither is ridiculous (although sometimes fun). The same logic applies to designing a house, picking a theme topic, buying a car, selecting a career or choosing a mate. If you don't make these decisions, someone (or the circumstances) will make them for you.

She loves me, she loves me not, she . . .

Now, about that problem of deciding which alternative is best. Consider the "best idea" as the missing piece of a jigsaw puzzle. The definition of the problem is your description of that missing piece. If your definition is very vague, general and nonspecific, it will apply to many pieces and make it impossible to select the best one. (The piece I'm looking for is sort of round with a couple of knobs protruding.) On the other hand, as your problem definition becomes more precise, you eliminate all incorrect pieces, because they don't fit your description of the best piece. Thus, the problem of selecting a plan of action is one of continually clarifying your objectives and goals (to get down to the real problem) until one alternative best balances the benefits and liabilities of the situation.

STEP 6. Do it

Don't fiddle around. Once you've decided what you want to accomplish, start immediately. How? Simple:

    a. Make a time table for the task

    b. Break very large projects down into a series of small steps. Treat each step as an important goal. Big goals can be overwhelming. Just chew a small bite at a time. (Don't forget to assign a time table for each of these pieces).

    c. Regard the whole process of implementing the idea as an experiment. It's not necessary for you to succeed with each idea. Experimentation is a cumulative, self-correcting process. Just learn enough so your next try will be an improvement.

Doing is learning.

Putting your ideas into action is the most important kind of learning experience. If you have high school or college teachers who encourage passivity by lecturing and giving only easy straightforward exams, they're doing you no favor. You're being shortchanged anytime you try to learn by letting someone else do your thinking for you, or by using your memory instead of your thinking ability.

There's an interesting experiment involving cats that points this up. It was found that cats who were chauffeured through a simple environment learned very little about it.[1] But, cats who were allowed to explore the environment on their own learned considerably more.

---

[1]Experimenter Marty Reisen in his famous "Case of the Chauffeured Cats."

Similarly, you will learn more about a particular route if you are driving the automobile rather than simply riding with someone else.

Acting on an idea gives you the opportunity to obtain meaningful feedback. And this is the basis for most learning. As we mentioned in Chapter 5, millions of drivers exhibit a high degree of skill and coordination during rush hour traffic because these skills were honed through continuous feedback. If high school and college learning were as finely controlled, we'd be a nation of geniuses. Remember, in order to receive feedback, you must be the actor — asking questions, exploring, speaking, designing, building.

STEP 7. Evaluate.

This is the test of the entire problem solving process. And it requires objective and impartial criticism. The key is answering the questions (a) did the solution accomplish my objectives? (b) if so, what improvements could be made? (c) if not, how would I solve the problem next time and why?

The most important part of an evaluation is not deciding whether the solution was successful. Most evaluations will be private affairs with only you aware of the real objectives, the solution, and the results. Evaluations are important because they tie the useful parts of a problem solving experience to your consciousness.

If you had dinner at many restaurants but never evaluated the quality or the price of the meals, you'd have no useful information for deciding where to eat in the future. So it is with problem solving. An honest evaluation summarizes what you have learned and want to remember. And, its purpose is to help you make correct decisions in solving similar problems in the future. It's easiest to make an honest evaluation when your goals are stated clearly. Then, it will be simple to decide whether the solution met your objectives. A vague goal (I want to improve my learning abilities) is impossible to evaluate until it is stated in concrete terms (I want to get an "A+" in Sex Education Lab).

The problem solving method we have covered is not fool-proof, nor is it the only good method. It can, however, with practice, make you a confident, efficient problem solver. You'll be doing this the rest of your life — setting goals, facing problems, finding solutions, putting them into action, and then evaluating your efforts.

And remember this: it is often more important to increase your understanding of the problem than it is to arrive at the best solution. Problems can be highly interrelated. Breaking off an unsatisfactory relationship may also turn "D's" into "B's" and get you to class on time.

You can't avoid problems unless you want to turn control of your life over to someone else. And that's the real reason why being skilled at problem solving is fundamental to a happy, fulfilling life.

Someone once told me that problems were just opportunities dressed up in a dirty word. But, then, he was only wearing a raincoat and carrying a sign that read "Argyle Socks Cause Cancer."

Chapter 11

Visual Thinking

The Magic of the Mind's Eye

You say you can't think your way out of a paper bag? You say you're about as creative as ten yards of carbon paper? You say you can't remember what your mother looks like? You say you have about as much control over your life as a greased bowling ball rolling down Mt. Everest? You say you have just won *Sports Illustrated's* "Klutz-of-the-Week" award for the ninth consecutive time?

Tell you what I'm going to do! Right here in this plain brown wrapper[1] is my special pair of Spectacular Spectacles designed to help you see with your mind's eye. Just slip them on and see way back to last year, get a clear shot of right now or peer into the unknown probabilities of the future.

Well, if it isn't ol' Snake Oil Sam back in his derby and checkered suit, gulling the corner crowd again. Come on out, Fenker. I'd know you anywhere. What are you hawking now? Peeping Tom lessons?

You don't need'em, Nurf.

No, this chapter is on Visual Thinking. Remember back in Chapters 2 and 3 we discussed the importance of visualization or imagery in performing many learning tasks? Well, now we are ready to define these "right-brained" skills in more detail and give you some exercises for improving your own visual thinking abilities.

Why bother? Because visual thinking is the key to improving your memory, your problem solving and comprehension skills, your creativity, your sports performance, plus your well-being and self-control. Quite a large order.

Wait a minute, Fenker. There's a federal law on the books called Truth in Packaging. And if you'll use a little visual thinking, you'll see Ralph Nader breathing right down your neck.

Just bear with me, Nurf. Let's take this one simple step at a time, and let me prove what I say. First of all, a definition. Visual thinking is thinking with pictures or images instead of words. It often involves three factors: (1) "seeing" which is

---

[1]Although such wrappers are more commonly associated with cheap whiskey, Dr. Fenker has been known to carry golf balls, peanut butter sandwiches, small sums of money and his wife in brown wrappers.

getting a correct visual perception of the world, (2) "imagining," which is creating mental pictures, and (3) "drawing," that is, expressing those ideas in some manner.

If these terms don't sound familiar it's because you've probably been short-changed in your education. In fact, unless you've been specifically trained as an artist or designer, the chances are good that you have not been given any formal schooling in these three areas.

Why? Because most of your classes are based on a model of education that is several hundred years old . . . and many years outdated. You were taught essentially the same verbal-analytical skills as your grandparents: reading, writing, speaking and mathematical reasoning.

This all results from the original purpose of education: to eliminate illiteracy. And anything which did not contribute directly to this goal, such as art classes or exercises in creativity or imaginative thinking, were (and often still are) regarded as frills. If these classes were offered at all, they were the first to be eliminated when the budget became tight.

But the purposes of education today go far beyond basic skills, especially at the level of high school or college. An education is both preparation for a job or career and the opportunity to develop a general awareness of the world, its history, peoples and cultures. It's the chance to grow personally and socially as well as intellectually. And, one of its major purposes is to add enjoyment and richness to your life.

Given this perspective, many things besides the "three R's" become important. These include areas such as creativity, problem solving, self-management or athletics. And your skills in each of these areas depends to some degree on visual thinking.

School curricula change very slowly, but there's no reason for you to wait another 50 years to learn about these vital aspects of a productive, happy life. We're going to have a go at them right now.

Visual thinking and perception

Almost every activity involves visual thinking to some degree: driving an automobile, talking with friends, reading, playing a sport, walking to class, planning, house-cleaning, etc. Clearly, every activity which involves visual perception also involves visual thinking.

But, there are other forms of visual thinking that have little to do with perception. *Memory images* are scenes of past events that can be pictured in your mind. Can you remember how your bedroom appeared when you were five, or the face of a friend not seen for years?

I can see him now, Uncle Godzillia. The green hair, the mustache, the 40" biceps. What a man!

Spare me your childhood memories, Nurf. Next there are images created by your imagination. These may contain elements of past or present images arranged in a new manner or different context. For example, you might imagine what your room would look like if painted white or what losing ten pounds would do for your waistline. Good problem-solvers or artists often generate and manipulate *imagination images,* much as a writer selects and organizes words.

Daydreaming or *fantasizing* is another form of visual thinking. In a daydream people visualize other people, objects or scenes which can be familiar or unfamiliar, known or unknown. Daydreams can be wish fulfilling dreams about work, stereo systems, sex or goal-directed exercises in problem-solving or creativity. Daydreams can be past, present or future-oriented.

Visual thinking has also had an impact on the language we commonly use to describe mental or decision-making processes. The visual origins are obvious for terms such as insight, foresight, hindsight, far-sighted, clairvoyant, clear; or for expressions such as "getting a better perspective," "seeing the whole picture," and "looking for a different point of view."

In the beginning/somebody talked

If you had been born, say on the 23rd of October, 9999 B.C., your world would have been dominated by visual consciousness. To primitive man, every plant, animal, mountain and thunderstorm was, in part, an expression of his inner reality, animated by forces within his mind. His everyday life was one conditioned by gods,

spirits and a variety of other mystical creatures. And often, his dreams and visions were indistinguishable from his perception of the world.

Then came the development of language. And with it, man began to separate his inner consciousness from external reality. Words became an abstract way of describing and manipulating objects as opposed to physically interacting with these objects. Man had discovered his ego-mind. And that mind was detached from the visual world which dominated his senses and from his body.

Little by little man separated his consciousness of the world from the world itself. He became an observer, skimming the crest of reality, his past history of survival quickly forgotten. With the development of moveable type, this detachment increased. It included not only words, but a system of thinking about the world known as rational or scientific thought. Man's language and mathematics allowed him to view not only objects but the interactions between objects in a detached, non-visual way.

Fascinating, Fenker. You've just covered thousands of years and gotten up to Gutenburg and Galileo. I can hardly wait to find out what happens next. Did Napoleon win? Did the Santa Maria sink?

You can catch the film at eleven o'clock to find out, Nurf. I was only pointing out that even with all of this passage of time, most learning skills books still reflect this detached, rational orientation. They offer a smorgasboard of techniques for controlling the external world — books, time, test performance, study behavior — without considering the world inside a learner's head.

Again, test your memory. You may recall I said earlier that one of the most important differences between visual thinking and thinking in words is that visual images represent "whole" complete concepts. Words only represent parts of the whole.

If you have to depend upon words to describe how a girlfriend or boyfriend looks, it can be a long, tedious and fairly inaccurate process. On the other hand, a photograph can communicate all this information and more in a single instant.

CUTE   BRUNETTE   BROWN EYES   BUILT

Thus "learning visually" means learning to see the parts in relation to the whole in one instant. That's why much problem solving or creativity depends on visual thinking. And one such combination of parts may be just the creative insight you were seeking. Such an occurrence usually generates the verbal response, "Ah-ha." Now do you see?

In order to understand how visual thinking aids problem solving and learning we need to examine how the brain combines parts into wholes. Let's begin with a straightforward statement about object perception. Notice the tree outside the window?

Yes.

You are seeing that tree with your mind, not your eyes.

Bless you, Fenker, you never disappoint me. I can always count on you to drop in some stupid remark like that. How do you know what my "mind" sees?

Because I know that your "eyes"[1] couldn't tell a tree from a Coor's beercan. All your eyes can do is break up the light reflected from the tree into a mosaic consisting of millions of tiny spots. It is the

---

[1]Dr. Fenker is actually referring to the retina of the eye which contains millions of light-sensitive cells known as rods and cones.

brain that decodes these spots into recognizable images as the information travels up the optic nerve.

Thanks a lot, Fenker. You really simplified things.

Now wait a minute, Nurf. My point is that what you end up seeing is the result of many organizing or "order-seeking" processes. Pick up a newspaper and look at a photograph. You see a face or scene. But if you put it under a magnifying glass, you'll see that it's made up of thousands of dots. Where the photograph is "black" you will find few or no dots at all. But your eye and your mind organize these patterns into grey tones. And you'll take a look and say, "Well, that's a picture of Alfred E. Newman rolling a joint!"

Similarly, visual thinking is an organizing or pattern-seeking process. Sometimes the organization is obvious, such as a checkerboard. More often, however, the correct pattern is only learned after our experiences help us filter out irrelevant information and focus on the critical details.

While it is possible to observe a scene that appears complicated or disorganized, it will be difficult to mentally visualize that scene until it obtains some degree of order. For example, try to form a mental picture of the instrument panel of a typical automobile. Easy; right? Now try the instrument panel of an airplane. Unless you're a pilot, your image will be vague and contain a variety of unknown or arbitrarily placed dials and meters. Most people have seen such airplane panels or pictures of them many times. But until you learn the function of each instrument and how they are organized, it's hard to form a coherent mental image.

Get it all together

In Gestalt psychology, there are several "grouping" laws which are descriptions of these pattern-seeking processes. They include:

1. **Good continuation.** This is the tendency to see a collection of dots or parts arranged in a sequence as if they were connected or forming the figure outlined by the sequence. The ancients did this with the stars, seeing all of the signs of the Zodiac as different arrangements of animals, objects or people.

2. **Similarity.** This is the tendency to group similar objects together. We see the red jerseys of one football team converging on the blue jerseys of the opponent's team.

137

3. **Proximity.** This is the tendency to see objects that are close together as forming groups. We tend to see clusters of trees, neighborhoods of homes, or mountain ranges — in other words, GROUPS of things — when they appear in close proximity.

(It's Gorbish's turn to give an example[1])

The Gestalt laws are important because the grouping processes they describe apply to visualization as well as seeing. Your subconscious mind is constantly organizing input and trying to make sense of the world in terms that fit your own personal needs. Its "solutions" may appear as images in dreams, daydreams, or in other forms of visualization. Thus, by using imagery for learning or problem solving you are bringing these powerful pattern-seeking processes into play.

Fenker, I think you have impressed your fellow psychologists quite enough for this chapter. How about a little low level communication with us peasants.

Let's not be testy, Nurf. Try an experiment. Take a deep breath and relax for a few seconds. Now close your eyes and attempt to form a mental picture of a special friend or loved one. Visualize their facial features in as much detail as possible. Got it? Is your picture clear or fuzzy and vague? Can you obviously "see" the image of your friend or must you "feel" or "sense" its presence?

Without special training and practice, most people report that their mental pictures are vague, unclear, soft and very dim compared to familiar visual perceptions.

A few people, however, are able to form images as clear and detailed as a photograph. These are called "eidetic" images. People who have this ability could re-draw a scene in great detail. Or, after glancing at this page, they could continue reading it by scanning their mental image.

I must have it, for I am visualizing Marilyn Monroe in minute detail.

How lucky for you, Nurf. You'll never be truly alone. You're probably good at another type of imagery — dreams. For many people, dream scenes are the most "real" of all images. And it's not unusual for the impression that a dream "actually happened" to extend into the waking state.

---

[1] You're so kind, Dr. Fenker. I've worked hard on this example. Notice the groups of words forming each paragraph on this page? Voila!

That explains this book. One nightmare after another.

Relax, Nurf, it's time for some magic. Let's first see how visual thinking can improve your learning ability; then, I'll give you some techniques for enhancing your imagery skills.

Here are some areas where visual thinking can help learners.

1. **Memory.** Visualizing material you want to remember helps establish the links that transfer information from short to long term memory. In Chapter 7, we discussed mnemonic linking systems which also depend on a connected sequence of visual images. (Remember the plane landing on the tree?) Both "meaningful" and "rote" memory tasks can be greatly improved by using visualization. It not only speeds the process of remembering new material, but it helps recall by providing another route for getting at the stored information.

2. **Problem Solving and Comprehension.** When we discussed these areas, we found that a critical factor was time. Time is necessary for comprehension so we can change or expand our view of the world to include new information. It takes time to arrange facts and alternatives into the best pattern for solving a problem. Visualization speeds both of these processes by permitting you to see all of the components of a problem simultaneously.

3. **Creativity.** Imagination is often used to describe the mental process on which creativity depends. It is largely a visual process, incorporating current images, daydreams or dreams and memories, rather than utilizing language.

Most systems for enhancing creative abilities depend on putting yourself in a receptive mood for "spontaneous visualizations" or "increasing the flow of inner images." Thus, as your skills in visual thinking improve so may your potential for creative ideas.

4. **Sports.** We'll cover this later. But for now accept this: visualization can improve your sports learning by communicating the appropriate patterns of movements to your muscles with pictures rather than words. Competitive performance can be improved by mentally rehearsing critical situations and in each case visualizing yourself making the appropriate actions.

5. **Self Control.** Earlier we saw the role of visual thinking in controlling everyday situations. The images we create of ourselves influence how we will think, behave and feel in the real world. And our skill at controlling internal distractors or self-monitoring as well as our overall attitudes about life can be influenced dramatically.

Fenker, you're casting your seed on concrete. With the exception of various portions of Marilyn, I have a blank screen. There's no use wasting time on improving my visual skills when I have no vision. My imagination is due for recall by Detroit.

Pish and tosh, Nurf. Everyone has an imagination that at least works in dreams or daydreams. Your problem is that you don't control or direct it toward a useful end.[1] This kind of control takes practice. But the ability to think imaginatively and to use visual imagery does not depend on the quality or realness of your images. It is only important that you practice using imagery often enough so you can consistently interpret your images, no matter how fuzzy or vague they are.

If, for example your image of a giraffe isn't a real picture, but just a blur or feeling of yellow and black, it will not affect the quality of your own visual thinking. The important thing is that you interpret the image consistently. I often interpret my visualizations by "feeling or sensing" them instead of "seeing" them as I would a photograph. Many people find that with practice the clearness improves and eventually your waking imagery can become as clear as the imagery in your dreams.

Okay, but you were talking about drawing and artistic talent. I have a tough time working a pencil sharpener.

Artistic ability is a learned skill like reading or writing or math. If the schools had spent as much time developing your ability to draw as they did on the three "r's," everyone would be an artist. You don't have to be artistic to think visually. And having good imagery doesn't imply artistic talent. Artists and designers usually possess both skills because they receive training in visual thinking, particularly the expression of visual ideas.

Okay, Okay. Don't get on your soap box again. Besides, you promised me techniques not talk.

Tuning your internal TV

Watch closely, Nurf. Off we go. Here's Fenker's Favorite Formula for Facilitating Fine Tuning. Before you begin the exercises, however, there are a few preliminary steps.

Before you begin

1. Find a quiet comfortable place where you are not likely to be distracted by other people, noises, the telephone or large animals.

2. Put yourself into a relaxed but alert state using the progressive relaxation method described in Chapter 2 (or any other technique appropriate for you).

3. When relaxed, concentrate your full awareness on the image or images you are using for the exercise. If distracting thoughts occur allow them to "drift" or "float" away. Do not focus your attention on them and they will quickly disappear.

4. Remind yourself each time you practice an exercise that the imagery you are

---

[1]An unfortunate choice of words, Fenker.

experiencing is becoming clearer and more vivid and that your ability to concentrate is growing stronger and more consistent.

5. Remember that visualization is a process that belongs to the *LISTENER*, not the *TALKER*. Self-talk most likely will interfere with your attempts to visualize.

In fact, if the *TALKER* interrupts one of your practice sessions, quite often the mental image you were "seeing" will quickly fade away. Negative thoughts about yourself or about the quality of the imagery are especially devastating. If that little voice is continually chastising you with negative feedback such as "I'm no good at this," "My imagery is as clear as mud," then, the *LISTENER* will respond accordingly. If self-talk occurs during visualization practice, don't "fight it" by actively resisting. Simply turn your attention back to the image.

Visualization exercises

1. Begin by visualizing colors. Fill your mind with red, green, blue, orange, or any other color you choose. Concentrate your full awareness on keeping the colors distinct and pure. If the colors your mind creates seem unclear to you (this is likely to happen until you have practiced the exercise several times) focus on the specific features that distinguish the colors from one another. How is red different from blue? Concentrate on this difference, study it, and the colors will become more distinct.

2. Next try visualizing familiar geometric shapes such as a circle, square or trian-

gle. First draw one of these shapes on a piece of paper and place it in front of you at eye level. Let your mind's eye study each part of the figure in detail then see the whole. Experiment by changing the size, shape or color of the object. Visualize the object rotating in your mind.

If you have difficulty with this exercise don't be disappointed or assume you are a poor visualizer. Some people find it much more difficult to image abstract shapes than objects or faces.

3. Now visualize a familiar three-dimensional object such as a chair, a ball, a tomato, a pencil or a cup. Position the image a few feet in front of you, relax, study the object then close your eyes and attempt to visualize it. Study the object's details and attempt to include these in your mental image. Now relax more deeply and allow your mind to create the image without critical evaluation or feedback from the *TALKER*.

4. Visualize a familiar person or animal. Concentrate on the face, studying each detail carefully. Now allow your mental perspective to shift and view the face from far away and then from very close. Next view it from the right side, the left side and finally the rear. Notice that visualizations are not limited by physical laws. You can move closer to an object or around it instantly.

5. Next visualize a familiar house or building. Imagine yourself opening the door and entering. Study the floor in front of you, the pictures and wall coverings in view and the entrances to other rooms. Allow your mind's eye to explore traveling

141

from room to room, noticing furniture, colors, windows and other details. Then, move back outside and explore the exterior of the house or building in the same careful manner.

6. Now visualize a pumpkin. That's right, a bright orange pumpkin with a stem on top. Imagine the pumpkin floating in front of you, rising slowly up to the ceiling. Let it sink back to eye level and begin to spin, faster and faster. Suddenly it stops and begins to grow smaller and smaller until it is the size of an apple. Now it changes colors and becomes bright blue, then green, then back to orange.

7. Imagine yourself lying comfortably on your bed. Mentally scan the room seeing familiar objects and furniture. Now repeat the scanning process but this time mentally move about the room viewing objects, furniture, windows and doors from up close. Now face the window and feel yourself floating gently toward it and passing through to the outdoors. Notice that you are drifting higher and higher until you are far above your neighborhood. Study the streets, houses, lawns, and trees from this perspective. Then drift gently back down to the earth, landing lightly on your feet.

8. Now visualize a very special place in your mind and imagine that you are in this place. The place might be a favorite vacation or scenic spot that you've visited before. It might be a place that you want to visit, or it can be an imaginary place that you create. It should be a place that is calm, restful and feels very pleasant. Explore this place in your mind. Examine your surroundings. Study their colors, shapes and textures. If it is outside, feel the warmth of the sun and the light breeze. Notice the smells and sounds. You may want to visit this special place many times in the future. Visualize yourself coming to this place to rest, to work on problems or to practice other exercises.

9. Visualize your "special place" and imagine meeting a very wise person or guide. Mentally picture yourself welcoming the guide and expressing your friendship.[1]

The guide may be a real or imaginary friend. Visualize yourself asking your guide to help you answer questions, solve problems or work on any task you choose. Listen carefully to what your guide tells you.

10. Finally, visualize another special place, your "workplace," which contains all the tools and instruments you might need to answer any question or solve any problem. Imagine a screen in the workplace where whatever images you choose can appear. Notice that your guide will visit you in the workplace whenever you need assistance. Practice seeing images of people and objects on your screen.

---

[1]Dr. Fenker failed to mention that many meditative or "mind control" schools offer training in imagery exercises similar to those described here. Also the use of hypnotic techniques can greatly speed the development of visualization skills.

Okay, but my screen keeps playing reruns of "Gilligan's Island" and commercials about bad breath and underarm tidiness.

These exercises are just a beginning, Nurf. But, if you will practice each one for approximately a week before going to the next, and use a relaxed state for this practice, I promise you impressive results in a few weeks.

Everyday imagery exercises

Here are a few other ideas for experimenting with visual thinking or improving your skills.

1. **After Image.** Take two brightly colored pieces of paper. Cut a triangle out of one piece and place it in the center of the other. Stare at the center of the triangle for 30 seconds, then quickly look at a blank white wall. You'll see the image of the triangle, but the color will be complimentary to the original hue.

2. **Retinal Excitation.**[1] Close your eyes (preferably in a dark room) and rub your eyelids very lightly or just apply slight pressure to them. This excitation of your retina will produce flashes of light. Try to organize them into meaningful patterns.

3. **Mental photography.** Pretend your mind is a Polaroid camera. Glance quickly at your surroundings, then close your eyes, and try to visualize the scene as clearly as possible. After some practice, try sketching the details of the scene. This is a helpful exercise for improving your ability to ''see'' the world in an unbiased manner.

4. **Reading with imagery.** Whenever you read, try to transform the dialogue into visual images. Create your own visual story or pictures to match the verbal statements. With practice, you can use this method to aid your memory for even abstract materials.

5. **Visual Association Frameworks.** These are such things as charts, organizational plans, maps, tables and diagrams. They provide a visual plan into which items to be remembered can be fit. These items then have a unique spatial relationship with other items, thus making recall easier.

6. **Dreams.** Try controlling your dreams. Just before you fall asleep, when you are in a relaxed state, tell yourself what you'd like to dream about. Also tell yourself that you will remember the dream upon waking. When you are dreaming, attempt to be conscious (in an everyday sense) within the dream without waking.

7. Read a book on games for the imagination such as Richard DeMille's *Put Mother on the Ceiling* or Richard Harris' *Mind Games.*

All of these will help sharpen your imagery abilities, and they're a heck of a lot fun, too.

---

[1] This is against the law in most states unless it occurs between two or more consenting adults.

I think I'm improving. I'm getting "Nova," "60 Minutes" and "Barth Gimble" on my screen with no commercials.

Great, Nurf. Now maybe you can work up to recognizing the individual faces in the Morman Tabernacle Choir.[1]

---

[1]Including those you don't know.

Chapter 12

Sports Learning

Stop Studying: Start Scoring

Okay, we're going to run through one of Fenker's Significant Scenarios. Lights, camera, action!

You're standing over your six-foot putt on the 18th hole. You're tied with your opponent, a poor winner, a blowhard, and you've never won a dime from him. You want to beat him so badly that you can almost taste it. You have a down hill lie, the toughest on the green. A helicopter is buzzing angrily toward the golf course. You take your stance, and feel the sweat from your forehead tickle as it runs down your nose. Your lousy opponent moves slightly within your peripheral vision. You pull the putter back and, as usual, he coughs, oh so unintentionally. You stroke the ball. It rolls smoothly in a lovely curve, hits the cup dead center and drops in.

Cut and print it.

Sound familiar? Can you imagine yourself performing well in a sport — making a crucial shot, catching a pass, winning a race? If so, then you have a headstart in becoming a good learner.

Hold it, Fenker. Come forward, and we'll roll the cameras again. I want to get a good shot of you accepting the award for the stupidest non-sequiter on an odd-numbered day. What has sinking a putt, with all of your B-movie theatrics, got to do with my physics test Friday?

Everything, Nurf. Why? Because the same kinds of skills that make good athletes also make good learners. And, the techniques presented in this book apply to both. I'm betting that you can master these learning strategies easier and quicker on the playing field than at your desk!

!!$$!![1]

All right, let me explain. Many of the skills necessary to be a good learner are just as necessary to be good in sports. Athletic training involves practice, concentration, self-discipline, strategies for dealing with distractors, memory, and so on. And don't forget time, effort and the

---

[1]Editors Note: Derogatory expletive deleted. This book is rated PG.

perseverance necessary to reach a long term goal.

Fine words, Fenker, but still unconvincing. I've almost finished this book, and I still don't expect to make the All-County Caber-Tossing Team.[1] This weighs heavily on my heart and may produce still another hernia in addition to the one I suffered in the semi-semi-finals.

I'm indebted to you for inadvertently making a good point, Nurf. Many people think that simply reading a book on learning will make them better learners. Hogwash! These same people would be the last to expect to become proficient at golf, tennis or caber tossing just by reading the instructions. Becoming skilled as a learner demands the same type of time and energy commitments you would expect to make in mastering a sport. The benefits

are, however, potentially unlimited. Unlike sports, which for most of us are weekend activities, you'll play some version of the learning game at school, work, or at home every day of your life. What keeps many people from becoming better learners is the following problem.

Becoming a good learner takes self-discipline and practice. And this can be tough when your practice-field is a desk covered with books on unpopular or difficult academic subjects such as history, mathematics or biology. But here is where athletics can be a big help. Because, believe it or not, the best place to develop your learning skills may be the athletic field, not the classroom. Why? Because the process of becoming a good learner has more in common with mastering a sport than it does with mastering geology or literature.

What does this process consist of? Well, a good coach or trainer will demand that you monitor how you are performing — your concentration, your technique, your mental attitude — instead of just whether or not you won. And it is this monitoring process, this concern with feedback, that is the key to improving.

The best part is that once you've mastered a sport and developed good concentration or self-monitoring skills, it's easy to apply them to study problems.

---

[1]Caber (kaa-b'r) — Young tree trunk used for tossing as a trial of strength in ancient Scottish sports. In the game's modern version, the tree trunk is greased and connected by a rope to the opponent's neck. Decapitated players are automatically disqualified. In the African version of cannibal-caber . . . .

Common ground

There is still a shadow of doubt in your mind? Then, let's go over these skills and see how they apply to sports and academics. And, in case you're wondering if I will continue to use golf examples, the answer is yes. I am a golfer. I admire Jack Nicklaus because of his skill, his devotion to the game, his true gentlemanliness, his grace in both victory and defeat and because he makes a potful of money.

1. Concentration. Learning to focus one's attention on a golf ball (okay, or on a mountain in skiing or on the track in road-racing) is similar to concentrating on a textbook. The old distractors are there — the movement, the cough, the helicopter or that little voice that says "You've never beaten this louse, and now that you have the chance you're going to blow it." Yet the effective learner or athlete is able to minimize such lapses in concentration.

Remember, in concentrating you simply focus your conscious energy on one thing, shutting out the sounds, smells, and sights around you. When you're really focusing, the headache disappears, the background music is silenced, and you don't think of Aureola at all. When a distractor appears you don't "fight it" by giving it your full attention. In-stead, you learn to ignore it by keeping your attention focused on the textbook or the fairway and letting the disturbance "drift" out of your awareness.

2. Feedback. I've suggested that you begin to control the process of learning by using relaxation and self-monitoring techniques. This same principle applies to sports learning. Becoming a good golfer involves more than shooting lower and lower scores. It requires learning in great detail about your swing, how it feels, what it looks like, and what effects various subtle changes in your stance or grip will produce. It involves a knowledge of the wind, sandtraps, and different kinds of grass. Understanding these factors help you control what happens on the golf course. But the key to achieving these kinds of control in sports or the classroom is practice plus feedback. Developing skills depends on monitoring how you are doing, then practicing to improve your performance.

3. Eliminating Bad Habits[1]: Improvement in sports or academics depends on replacing bad habits with good ones. The behavioral management strategies offered in

---

[1] I would wager that Dr. Fenker is about to begin another long-winded repetition of behavior management strategies.

149

Chapter 4 work well in both areas. Enough said.[2]

4. Challenge and the Fear of Failure: Both academics and athletics are challenging endeavors that offer unlimited opportunities for growth. Yet, many people are unable to achieve their full potential in such situations. Why? Because fear of failure, anxiety about competition or destructive self-talk programs cause them to freakout. But often it takes a challenge to provide the incentive for an athlete or learner to reach full potential. Swimmers, runners and Caber tossers seldom set records unless they are pushed by good competition. You can probably remember a teacher who pushed you to the limit. You may have grumbled about the hard work and the unfairness of it all, but there was a warm, rich feeling of satisfaction when you recognized how well you were doing.

5. Visual Thinking: As we've seen, visual thinking is important to many learning processes, memory, concentration, comprehension, and creativity. It's also vital for successful performance in athletics. The physical part of sports is largely a "right-brain" activity. And the right-brain learns much more effectively with images or pictures than with words.

A movie of Jack Nicklaus swinging a golf club lasts only a few seconds. Yet, it would take a small book to describe in words what took place in that short time.

Or, imagine trying to tell a centipede how to walk, "Look, Sam, first you move your No. 1 leg on the right side, and just as you are raising it — just about so — you start raising the No. 1 leg on the left side, but don't rush it — not too soon — and then you start raising your No. 2 leg on the right side. . . ."

Fenker's Famous and Final Disclaimer

Are you ready for some specific techniques for improving your athletic skills?

Hold on, Fenker. I'm still not convinced that this crazy sports chapter will improve my academics. I've been tossing the caber for nigh onto three years, and I still got an "F" in my favorite class last semester, "The Economics of Cheese Straightening."

All right, Nurf, then answer these questions. How seriously did you toss the caber? Did you ever really try to concentrate? Did you learn to appreciate and monitor the process of balancing the caber? Did you study the sequential contrac-

---

[2]Okay, so I was wrong.

tion of the proper muscles for maximum distance? Huh, Nurf Did you? You had your chance to do this each time you picked up the caber, but you just tossed it away.[1]

It is possible that your sports activities will not help your academics. That's okay. If this chapter helps only with sports, it will be successful from my standpoint.[2] But if you're serious about mastering a sport, and learn to perform it well, I predict your concentration, monitoring and self-management skills will also improve in the classroom. Let's get on with the major purpose of the chapter: to give you the tools for increasing your mastery of a sport.

Practice, Practice, Practice

Two of the requirements for becoming a superior athlete are obvious. And you can find them listed in any sports book. These are:

1. **Physical conditioning.** You just don't buy a $150 set of racquetball togs and a racquet, sign up for a $500 membership in a club and start tearing the walls down with driving serves into the corner. Each sport has its own set of guide-lines for improving muscular conditioning, coor-

dination, and stamina. And you can find excellent books on these for each particular sport. But, remember, mental activities seem to require the same kind of conditioning, so be prepared to do both.

2. **Practice.** This is another requirement. Shooting a basket, hitting the pocket between the one and three pin, swimming the length of the pool and making a quick turnaround all consist of a series of complex actions. And considerable practice is necessary to make them efficient, powerful and accurate. Practice serves to "program" the right brain with the appropriate action sequences. And it produces the physical coordination necessary to make these sequences automatic.

The next requirement is also obvious, but its meaning is more elusive.[3]

Appropriate mental attitude

Marvelous, Fenker, for someone who insists on exact definitions and quantifying everything in sight, appropriate mental attitude has the preciseness of a handful of grits. Whaddaya mean?

---

[1]Dr. Fenker, I believe that is the idea: to just toss it away — a long way.

[2]The standard English version of the expression Dr. Fenker has so cleverly disguised in academic double-talk is "cop-out".

[3]If it was elusive to begin with, then by the time Dr. Fenker finishes it will be totally incomprehensible.

Well, to be honest, I'm not sure. The pro at the club where I learned to play golf in high school was always saying, "You'll be a great golfer when you're older if you can just develop the proper mental attitude." For years I read various golf books looking for tips. I found that aside from such suggestions as, "concentrate" or "think positively" or "don't let a bad hole shake you," there were as many different mental attitudes as there were authors.

Some writers suggested golfers should always remain relaxed or "loose". For others a moderate amount of tension was crucial. Some focused on maintaining a competitive drive or the "winning edge". And still others ignored all external conditions and concentrated on the "process" of swinging the golf club.

Me? I say your best mental attitude is a unique blend of your own personality and the requirements of the sport. But, there are several features of a "good mental attitude" common to most if not all sports. What are these?

- Self-confidence
- A desire to win or perform well
- Positive self-talk programs
- Maintaining an optimal level of tension or stress[1]
- Clear separation of thinking and non-thinking activities

Non-thinking activities?

Exactly! In fact the most important mental activity in sports is probably non-thinking.

Marvey! I'm going to be a star and sign autographs, endorse products and make TV commercials. Fenker, you may be my agent and carry my caber from meet to meet.

Now, wait a minute, Nurf. When I say "non-thinking," I'm not talking about a native full-blown talent in this area such as you have. I'm talking about silencing the TALKER so that negative thoughts about yourself, the circumstances, your opponent, your past performance or what could or could not happen to you don't effect your actions. If you catch yourself saying:

"My backhand is a disaster. I'll never be able to return her serve."

"I missed that last field-goal by a mile. I'll probably miss this one as well."

"I can't face my friends if I lose this match."

"There's a pond in front of the green and a sandtrap on the other

---

[1]Dr. Fenker failed to mention that optimal tension levels vary considerably for different athletes and sports. Many athletes need to relax in order to achieve this optimum level; however, many others have to increase their tension or stress in order to perform well.

side. This shot is doomed."

"She's the state champion. I can't compete with her."

"I've been missing easy shots all night. Why doesn't the coach take me out?"

Then, these negative statements become part of the information sent from your brain to your muscles. They become images or instructions for your muscles to execute!

Ideally, an athletic "action" (e.g., a swing or stroke, a block or kick, a shot or serve, a jump or dash, a catch or throw) is an unconscious event. It's an automatic process, controlled by the right-brain, in which your muscles perform a coordinated sense of movements. What happens if the *TALKER* participates in this process immediately before or during the activity? Most likely the participation will interfere with performance.

Why? Because the programs for performing at your best are already stored in your muscles and right-brain. All you have to do is allow them to operate at the appropriate times. And you can do this best by "non-thinking" in the usual verbal manner. Self-talk, particularly negative self-talk, interrupts these automatic programs by transmitting tightness to muscles that should be relaxed.

Timothy Galloway describes this process well in his book on the *Inner Game of Tennis:*

Let's take a closer look at this

tightening process because it is a phenomenon which takes place in every athlete in every sport. Anatomy tells us that muscles are two-way mechanisms; that is, a given muscle is either relaxed or contracted. It can't be partially contracted any more than a light switch can be partially off. The difference between holding a racket loosely and tightly is in the number of muscles which are contracted. How many and which muscles are actually needed to hit a fast serve? No one knows, but if a conscious mind thinks it does and tries to control those muscles, it will inevitably use muscles that aren't needed. When more muscles than necessary are used, not only is there wasted energy, but certain tight-end muscles interfere with the need for other muscles to stretch. Thinking that it has to use a lot of muscle to hit as hard as it wants to, self one (the left hemisphere) will initiate the use of muscles in the shoulder, forearm, wrist, and even face which will actually reduce the force of the swing.

Clearly, there is a "thinking" part of sports: where to place a serve; what play will fool the defense; what club the shot requires; how to ski a mountain. But normally this kind of verbal reasoning precedes the activity. Once the physical part of a serve, shot, play, kick, etc. has begun

153

non-thinking is the key. So, remember: Don't let the *TALKER* create unnecessary tension. Keep your earplugs in.

The next requirement for becoming a skilled athlete is knowing how to change your behavior with feedback or behavioral management strategies.

Behavior Management: The ability to change one's behavior is obviously as important in sports learning as it is in academic learning. The techniques we learned earlier in Chapter 4 apply directly to sports learning.

    a. **Examine the present behavior,** decide what's wrong and what you would like to change: I enjoy hitting practice balls at the golf driving range, but it seems that I never find the time to practice putting. Unfortunately, putting is the weakest part of my game.

    b. **State your objectives** in clear behavior terms: I want to spend at least 30 minutes of every golf practice session working on my putting game.

    c. **Design a behavior system** that will accomplish your objectives: I'll use the Premack principle. Since hitting irons and woods is enjoyable and a high probability behavior, I'll make it contingent on putting practice. The system: 30 minutes on the practice green before any longer shots.

    d. **Implement the system:** This was the easiest part! Every day for two weeks I putted, then hit practice balls.

    e. **Evaluate your system:** It worked great! My putting improved considerably. I even began to look forward to putting practice.

    f. **Feedback** or improvements needed in the system: None.

This procedure works well for many athletes. However, I offer two cautions.

First, in team sports, behavioral management is often complicated by the presence of other people or circumstances beyond your control. In general, do not develop a behavioral system that depends on extensive cooperation from others or unrealistic circumstances.

Second, it's often difficult to simulate the feelings of pressure and tension in practice which influence your performance in an actual event. If your efforts in practice are not paying off in competitive situations you might try one of the scenario methods described below. Or, you might relax on the white line of a freeway to produce some tension.

Fenker's Award Winning Drama in Real Life —

    Grant was a member of TCU's varsity basketball team. He had the talent to be a regular starter but his playing was so erratic that he spent most games on the bench. Grant blamed his poor play on problems with the coach. When criticized by the coach during practice, Grant's normal reaction was anger and self-defeatism. He'd say, "Why bother to improve. The coach will always find fault with what I do." Then his play would become lethargic and irregular.[1]

When he came to me for help he'd been suspended, for the second time, from the team.

After some discussion, Grant confessed that the coach was probably not really "out to get him" but was only trying to help him improve. His sensitivity to any sort of critical feedback, however, ruined what might otherwise be opportunities for learning and self-improvement.

The behavior program Grant and I designed focused on this one key issue: Viewing the coach's criticism as a positive rather than a negative event. We first developed a set of positive self-talk statements[2] that were initiated by a critical remark from the coach. We then set-up a simple behavioral system that rewarded Grant for receiving criticism or feedback and responding constructively. In fact, Grant was encouraged (by the system) to ask for feedback.

The results? Even I was surprised. By the end of the season, Grant was not only playing regularly but was the star attraction. He was later named to the all conference team!

Are you making all of this up Fenker? We haven't had a player on the all-conference-team in 20 years. They've all been on scholastic probation.

Not since I wrote this book Nurf. Keep reading. The final techniques are the most powerful of them all.

Visualization: The use of visualization or imagery techniques in sports is not new. The Eastern Europeans and Russians have been doing it for the past two decades. But it is only very recently that such techniques have received much attention in the United States. Most applications of imagery are based on a complex psychological law: Monkey see, monkey do.

Now wait just a minute, Fenker.

My apologies Nurf. Just trying to keep the discussion at your level. As we discussed both in Chapter 11 and earlier in

---

[1] We recommend Carter's Little Liver Pills.

[2] In case you're interested, I have a couple of these filed in my memory: 1) "Good, the coach is showing concern for me by giving helpful feedback"; 2) "Excellent, I have another opportunity to develop my skills;" 3) "I have the most potential of any player on the team. That's why the coach is so concerned about my improvement."

Chapter 3, imagery is the language of the right-brain. And the right-brain is responsible for coordinating the automatic sequences of physical activity required for most sports. Thus, the key to rapid sports learning or championship performance is imagery. Why? Because by creating a mental image of what you want to happen you accomplish two important things. First, you help eliminate the distracting conversation of the *TALKER*; and, second, you communicate your goals or instructions directly and instantly to the right-brain.

Let's see how these principles might apply to sports learning. Assume that you're a skier struggling to master parallel turns. Your instructor suggests you use your knees instead of your upper body to provide the turning action. Before you begin the next run you sit quietly for a few moments and visualize yourself turning using an exaggerated knee action. Or, you visualize the instructor (or any good skier) making the turn correctly. Rehearse this action several times because this procedure tells the right-brain "how your knees should move" when you make the next turn.

Now, off you go down the mountain, visualizing the appropriate knee-action, but not using self-talk instructions. Once the *TALKER* begins, an avalanche[1] of distracting thoughts is likely to follow: "Let's

see, do I shift my weight from the inside ski out to begin a turn, or is it from the outside ski in? Wow, this hill is steep. Whoops, watch out for the pole of that buried skier. The wind sure is gusty. Knees bent, shoulder pointing down hill. Now, turn and twist those knees! There's a tree!!" SPLAT!

Such thought sequences create tension in certain muscles that interfere with your naturally coordinated movements. My own peak skiing experiences came when I could shut down all thinking and only feel. And this often occurred when I was following an instructor or other good skier down a slope and visually duplicating his or her movements.

That must explain it. The other day I was following this gal down the street, observing closely her every moment. And a guy came up and asked me for a date.

Remember to relax

Now, let's examine some specific methods for improving your sports performance using imagery. Remember, imagery exercises are much more effective if performed while you're in a relaxed or meditative state. So find a quiet place, use the progressive relaxation technique described in Chapter 3, then use the appropriate imagery exercise.

---

[1]Clever, Dr. Fenker. Very clever, but actually an avalanche is defined as a sudden great or overwhelming rush of snow and other materials down a mountainside. Just like this book, it's a giant "snow-job".

a. **Modeling is marvelous.** In many sports, instructors try to teach you a complicated series of movements part by part: address the ball (howzit going, ball?) swing your club back slowly, shift your weight, keep your left arm stiff, turn your shoulders, etc. This is ridiculous! Not only are "words" a very poor language for describing a complex series of muscular actions; but, it's next to impossible to master separate actions and them combine them into a smooth, coordinated sequence.

A more effective method of learning that has proved popular in tennis, skiing and golf is *modeling*. Here's how it works. First you watch a very good athlete performing the actions you'd like to master; let's say a tennis serve. You can do this by observing them in person, or by substituting TV or movies. Next, attempt to visualize and remember the tennis stroke, golf swing or other action. Create a motion picture for your mind, it's worth tens of thousands of words. And, this process works even if your imagery is abstract and not very clear.

Practice comes next. Remember to relax, then mentally rehearse the imagery you have learned. You might continue to visualize the good athlete performing the serve (or other action) or visualize yourself serving in the same manner as the good athlete. Repeat your practice sessions daily for at least two weeks. Then, test your learning where it counts — on the sports field. The results will astonish you, I promise.

b. **Pseudo-practice.** This is similar to modeling except it's often used to rehearse a well-learned activity, not develop new skills. Pseudo-practice is mental rehearsal of a sports activity using imagery. Thus, a football player might imagine himself blocking, tackling or catching passes. A baseball player might imagine herself hitting or fielding.

I regularly use pseudo-practice to keep my flying skills sharp. I imagine practicing a consistent glide, holding the airspeed steady, breaking the glide at just the right height, holding the plane off the ground as the speed decays and touching down with the nose high. I may shoot a dozen landings in my mind. And invariably, on my next flight, I find it has helped.

c. **Scenario.** This involves imagining probable events that might confront you in an athletic contest and then imagining how you would respond to these events in an ideal fashion. In other words, you're anticipating the things that are likely to occur and rehearsing how you want to deal with them. It's especially useful for problems or situations that occur so infrequently you are not likely to have practiced the correct response.

Some examples of scenarios[1] are:

1. Baseball: An infielder might rehearse his responsibilities for when there are men on base. He'll plan what to do if the ball is hit on the ground or in the air.

2. Basketball: A basketball player might rehearse the different plays used during the game. She would visualize her actions on each play for various defensive arrangements.

3. Tennis: A tennis player might rehearse scenarios for some of the unusual shots that opponents hit occasionally in matches. Shots that tip the net, lobs over the head, unorthodox serves, or shots with excessive spin are good examples.

Fenker's Award Winning Drama in Real Life — *The Resurrection of Ralph!*

One of my students who "benefited" from scenario practice was a football player named Ralph. Ralph was a 270 pound freshman tackle. Although he had learned the plays without difficulty, he was often confused by the special situations that occurred during games. Audibles, unusual defensive formations and last minute substitutions occasionally confused Ralph and caused mistakes.

To begin, I had Ralph list the situations that he found most confusing. Then he worked out a brief scenario for each situation, imagining himself performing correctly each time. After three weeks of rehearsing the scenarios Ralph was given

[1]Dr. Fenker's favorite scenario is one in which he is standing on a corner, a gorgeous blonde in silver Mercedes stops, opens the door, asks him to get in and presents him with a wallet containing $20,000 in large bills, inquiring if it is his? It hasn't happened yet, but Dr. Fenker is prepared.

the starting position at right tackle. Four plays later he was out for the season with a broken collarbone.[1]

d. **Butterflies beware:** It is not uncommon for athletes to "freak out" in competitive situations because of tension or anxiety about performing well. One form of "freak-out" occurs when your mind is bombarded by all of the negative events that might occur (and usually do if you expect them to). Another version occurs when the pressure to perform is so great it interferes with or inhibits your movements. Even professional athletes will occasionally lose their concentration in pressure situations. And the tightening of the wrong muscles is the likely result.

Scenario practice is excellent for eliminating "butterflies" due to negative thoughts or pressure. During the week before a competition achieve a relaxed state, then imagine yourself overcoming the negative possibilities that might occur. Or imagine yourself being aware of the pressure but performing well anyway. A sports psychologist or your coach can help you design these exercises and perhaps even prepare a special tape to help you rehearse.

e. **Real time imagery programs:** So far we've only discussed how imagery might be used in practice sessions. Well, it can also be used effectively during compe-

tition in many sports like golf, tennis, skiing, bowling, basketall, swimming or baseball where the action is not continuous. How? Well, before each swing, serve, descent, ball, foul shot, dive or strike, imagine yourself performing correctly. Visualize the tee shot's trajectory in your mind and see it land squarely in the center of the fairway. Imagine serving the tennis ball with a smooth, powerful swing and see the ball zip over the net and bounce just inside the baseline. For each of the other sports simply spend a second or two visualizing yourself making the appropriate action. Then go do it! The results will amaze you.

Fenker's own sports saga

Tired of hearing about golf? So am I. Let's try a baseball example. For the past several years I've played for a "slow-pitch" softball team known as the PSY-CHLONES. I'm an average fielder and until recently, an even more average batter. But this past summer I used the real-time imagery technique described above. A minute or two before it was my turn to bat I would close my eyes and imagine taking a level swing at the ball, making good contact. You won't believe how well it worked. My average last year was .263. This year it was .740!

You're right, I don't believe it.

---

[1] A scenario he had not practiced.

f. **Affirmations:** What's an affirmation? It's a self-talk statement about something you would like to do or become that you make to yourself on a regular basis. Examples are "I'm going to be the fastest free-style swimmer in the state" or "My strength and endurance are improving daily" or "I am the strongest powerlifter in my class" or "My concentration is excellent." Many coaches and athletes have discovered the power of affirmations plus imagery. You become what you affirm through words and imagery. If you tell yourself you are improving, then visualize this improvement. You'll improve. Just try it!

For best results, select a regular time-period for repeating your affirmations. In the morning just before waking, during a mid-day relaxation period or in the evening just before retiring are excellent times. Enter a relaxed, right-brain state, then begin your affirmations, visualizing what you want to become. Keep your thoughts positive and realistic but don't be afraid to set high goals for yourself. Avoid negative thoughts because this process works both ways. And before you realize it you'll "be" what you imagined.

Nearing the end

Learning in sports and learning in academics are very similar processes. In both cases practice, concentration and a strong desire to improve are essential. And when you have the chance to apply what was learned, on an examination or in athletic competition, remember to keep

your mind in the present tense — relaxed but aware — and be willing to use your potential to the fullest.

You have now virtually completed this book. But again I remind you, reading it is just the first step. It has offered you a myriad of techniques, methods and strategies for making the learning process more efficient and more effective. They're like an array of artist's brushes from which you can choose the one with the right length, balance, texture, and size to accomplish a particular need. Many are novel to you and will open exciting new doors to learning. Others are old friends that perhaps have been sharpened and improved from my reminders.

Remember, learning is an individual process, so select those tools which fit you best, those which can answer your specific problems, and those with which you feel most comfortable. And allow time for practice, for most of us have many years of neglect and disuse to overcome.

But, if you want to greatly improve your capacity as a learner, it's the best investment you can make. It's the key to a whole new world of mental development and will also enhance many of the strategies presented in this book. Improvement won't happen overnight, but, with some persistance, you will get results. Marvelous results. Measurable results. I promise you that!

I'm sure that most people who pick up this book and start to read it will react much as Nurf did. But I hope by now your skepticism (or some of it) is gone.

Not so fast, Fenker. I'm still not sure it will work for me.

Look at it this way, Nurf: It will work for you if you will work for you. It's your responsibility now. You cannot blame your roommate, your TV, your teachers, your books or even Aureola any longer. Those problems are still there, and they'll remain there, but you now have the tools to conquer them.

That is a sneaky, lousy trick to play on anyone.

You're learning, Nurf, you're learning!

Richard M. Fenker Jr., a native of Gallatin, Tennessee, is a professor of psychology at Texas Christian University in Fort Worth, Texas. He holds degrees from the Case Institute of Technology and Purdue University. For many years he has offered classes in "Learning Skills" to high school and college students. This book represents a collection of his most effective methods.

TEXT SET IN 10 POINT PALATINO
BY TYPE CASE
AND PRINTED BY EVANS PRESS
FORT WORTH, TEXAS